◆

Scratching and stirring up desire are typical
tasks of the kind of research that stains the
fingers of our souls.

mpT

MODERN POETRY
IN TRANSLATION

The best of world poetry

No. 1 2022

© *Modern Poetry in Translation* 2022 and contributors

ISSN (print) 0969-3572
ISSN (online) 2052-3017
ISBN (print) 978-1-910485-32-3

Editor: Clare Pollard
Managing Editor: Sarah Hesketh
Digital Content Editor: Ed Cottrell
Finance Manager: Deborah De Kock
Design by Brett Evans Biedscheid
Cover art by Priyanka D'Souza
Typesetting by Libanus Press

Printed and bound in Great Britain by Charlesworth Press, Wakefield
For submissions and subscriptions please visit www.modernpoetryintranslation.com

Supported using public funding by
**ARTS COUNCIL
ENGLAND**

MODERN POETRY IN TRANSLATION

The Fingers of Our Soul:
The Bodies Focus

CONTENTS

Focus

Reviews

EDITORIAL

By Khairani Barokka and Jamie Hale,
guest editors of this issue's focus

Welcome to the special Bodies Focus of *Modern Poetry in Translation*. In sifting through the many remarkable submissions we received, we have been privileged to read a plenitude of poetries that expand our understandings of the vessels we live in. Poems that can, with a single word, create a new framework for living. Verse in which bodies of various creatures interact and refract so many emotions and prisms for the corporeal.

Creating this, we want to thank our access assistants, family, friends, and partners, the team at *Modern Poetry in Translation*, DL Williams, Priyanka D'Souza for the stunning cover design, Salma Harland for the prose piece on Abū al-ʿAlāʾ al-Maʿarrī's poetry, Raka Nurmujahid for a commissioned translation from Bahasa Isyarat Indonesia (Indonesian Sign Language or BISINDO), Anthony Price for a translation between computerised Englishes using eyegaze computer input, and too many others to name.

As we selected translations, we worked through a range of embodiments, looking for pieces that explored the universality of our shared existence within bodies, balanced with the divergent experiences of individual bodyminds. We chose pieces reminding us that we as vulnerable bodies experience the world in such vastly varied circumstances – that the subtleties of feeling are so unique to each person, shaped by socio-political landscapes in flux. We recognise the persistent inequities in terms of accessibility for d/Deaf and disabled writers across the world, and hope this issue will spark further, systemic change in publishing and translation.

Here you will find powerful verse on deep bodily grief, and the intensities of violence, alongside humorous pieces that poke and prod at the playfulness of physical existence. These poems 'waltz langvalourously | Come and go velvetvolleying on the paper' – as in Stephanie Papa's translation of Levent Beskardès.

There is work translated from a range of signed languages, bringing with it visual interpretations of works performed in motion. We wanted to create within an ethos of equality between sensorial modes, and welcome the opportunities to explore and experiment with publishing varying presentations.

We have distinctly privileged D/deaf and disabled poetics, being disabled ourselves, living in a time of genocides against the most vulnerable. Through these poems and translations we reach towards an understanding of d/Deaf and disabled experiences, reflecting an engagement with the form and limitation of the corpus – both as human body, and body of poetic work.

Ultimately, survival, living, and deep care for the world pulse through the poems we selected here, forming the veins of this issue. We hope they speak and sign to you with, as poet Àngel Terron says, and Rafael Cruz translates, 'the fingers of our souls'.

Khairani Barokka and Jamie Hale

GEET CHATURVEDI

Translated by Anita Gopalan

The poem 'Letters from a Kashmiri Boy' by Geet Chaturvedi, a Hindi poet, thinks with images, building a balance between language and sensation. The small boy's simple observations, and his sufferings addressed (implicitly and variously) to terrorists or the government or himself, speak of a keen intellect and sensitivity. The poet's own harrowing experience of terror and pain found voice when, as a teenager during the Mumbai terror attacks of 1992, he witnessed his elder sister dying, with no doctor around amid curfew. There is a simplicity in the language that brings forth the poignancy, touching the common reader. The translation expands at times on the original to make a particular regional nuance clearer as well as to create the energy and rhythm.

SOME NOTES: Dal lake mentioned in the poem is in Kashmir and geographically lies to the north of New Delhi. Laladyad and Abhinavagupta were Kashmiri mystic-poet-philosophers. Ney is a reed flute played by the Sufis, the sound of which is believed to resonate the love of God.

Letters From a Kashmiri Boy

I

My brown body has blackened.
It's not the burn of sun.
The shadow of Truth has fallen on it.

The sacred texts and the Sufi ney,
Laladyad and Abhinavagupta –
All filled with Truth.

I'm not near worthy enough to bother.

My lamb descended not from Mount Arafat
but from the Himalayas.
Moments before the sacrifice
I put my mouth to her ear and said,
        'Truth is not hidden under the rumps of philosophy.
        It is like the vampire hanging on a tree:

        that we spend so many lives only to live
        on a piece of land, fight
        for a piece of land, and
        die for it.

        This is our piety.'

Opposite: A smiling man in a white t-shirt and a grey beanie looks into
the camera, with his arms crossed. He is indoors. Behind him are a
framed pair of illustrated portraits of suited men.

The generous lamb forgave her slayers.
Content filled her as she died
saint-like
without curses or tears.
Truth had laid its shadow on her.

If you must know who I am,
I am the lamb of this land.

II
Echoes are louder
than the sounds that form them
    and last a lifetime.

Here, and all that is beyond
snow and mud
my cry resounds
in the open valley

flung onto the slippery earth
takes a flower's name.

Now I understand
why Kashmir is swamped by flowers.

III
I am the meaning
of the sentence
that got blown up by a fucking bomb.

I am the nameless pronoun
for a voice
that was whapped by bullets.

I am the curfew's siren
that soothes a pounding heart.

I am the tail-wagging silence
of a friendly stray dog
patient on the doorstep. Silence
that licks the wounds of voices stripped naked and lashed.
Silence like an inky shadow
that lengthens slowly.

I was born, just as you,
a love letter addressed to the world.

I live, like a paper boat
rustling on bloodied waters
not knowing
which government office I should go to
seeking permission
to live as a human.

IV
You say, Dal Lake is in the north
and I say, it is south of me.
The only difference between us lies in
where we are standing.

I and you: different humans
but equal human souls
and our humanity is the same.

Strike at my humanity,
annihilate it and your own
will become meaningless.

V
I am a laboratory rat
for my god and my government.

My heart is a black hole,
roofless enclosure.
I feel no shame when I see
how deep into it my darkness sat.
Then.

A hand-grenade. Its blunt head ready to explode.

Saying *Attention, people*
    God's fallen asleep. The world
    spins on auto-pilot.
    Wear tight your hope.

My darkness stares
from the ramparts.

Your valley won't change – still,
you seek the paradise lost in it
and this will be given. Take it
at the profound moment when you die.

DU FU

Translated by Andrew Neilson

The poets Du Fu and Roddy Lumsden wouldn't normally be paired together in the mind, but there's no accounting for grief. Du Fu (712–770) is widely regarded as the greatest of the classical Chinese poets. Roddy Lumsden (1966–2020) was a Scottish poet, teacher and editor, whose passing just before the pandemic was much felt in the UK poetry scene. As one of Roddy's oldest friends in poetry, I found myself revisiting this lyric after he died. It speaks to a certain melancholy, and considerations of art and life, which seemed germane.

'Winding River' (one of two poems by Du Fu with the same title) dates from a period when the poet served briefly as a minor functionary, a 'Reminder', in the Tang imperial court. Du Fu's career was cut short in the summer of 758 when he was arrested for attempting to defend a patron in trouble with the law. It is likely that 'Winding River' was composed during his final months at court.

Du Fu's 'regulated verse' consists of eight lines of seven pictograms each, paired as couplets. It is highly formal, utilising both rhyme and complex tonal patterning. As a result, most translations of Du Fu eschew rhyme and metre as there is no directly parallel way of rendering his poems into traditional English forms. My version attempts to communicate something of the formality by rendering the eight lines as four short ballad-like stanzas, with each stanza representing a couplet of the original.

Winding River

Spring fades with each blossom
flying in the wind.
Ten thousand points now float,
grief and beauty limned.

Passing is the petal,
fallen are my eyes.
Only wine, a skinful,
will see my gaze rise.

The hall by the river,
a kingfisher's nest,
the hall which is a tomb
where unicorns rest.

Joy is the only law
worthy of study.
What use immortal fame
to mortal body?

SHOOKA HOSSEINI

Translated by Farzan Sojoodi, Alireza Abiz and Zack Rogow

Born in 1982 in Tehran, Shooka Hosseini belongs to the generation
that experienced war and political unrest, witnessed public funerals
of fallen soldiers, and took part in protests in streets and on
campuses. She started writing poetry in her teens while the country
was undergoing major political and social transformations that
shaped her character as a rebellious woman and an outspoken poet.
Hosseini writes boldly: her sharp unreserved tone, erotic and feminist
approach, and mastery of form have brought her recognition among
the literary circles in Iran and throughout the Persian-speaking
world. She has studied Persian literature, linguistics, and psychology.
Hosseini works in Tehran as a psychotherapist. She is also a
performance artist, writes book reviews and literary criticism,
and has gained a reputation as a theatre critic.

'The Streets inside My Head' is a multi-layered poem blending
personal memories with historical facts in a highly charged narrative
about contemporary Iran and the wider Middle East. The poet walks
us through the cities of her dreams, which are like palimpsests where
ruins of ancient civilisations meet contemporary metropolises prone
to destruction in modern-day conflicts. The emotional depth,
spontaneous imagery, heightened lyric quality, and rapidly shifting
landscapes excite me every time I read this poem, but those same
qualities made it a challenge to translate. I told Shooka Hosseini that
I intended to translate this poem into English and she sent me a draft
translation by Professor Farzan Sojoodi to work on. I made many
changes, but wasn't happy with the outcome, so asked Zack Rogow
to help. It took us a couple of Zoom meetings and many exchanges
of emails until we were content that we had a version we can happily
share with readers of English.

The Streets Inside My Head

Many streets walk inside my head
Streets with grey benches
With poplar trees like my heart – and where is my heart?
With a little daddy plucked from my memories
With a sad doll tucked under my dress, walking hand in hand with
      the gloomy wind
Many streets walk inside my head
Passersby wave to me,
To the white shirts of apathy, and maybe to something flickering far
      away? No, not to that.
To the cobblestone streets sometimes covering ancient clay tablets
And the footprints of pedestrians
To parallel lines of cars cars cars cars
When I don't follow the rules for crosswalks and I forget that
These lines are just to die more efficiently
Many streets walk inside my head
Hand in hand with many other cities
The cities of my dreams, where every day I dug your corpses out of
      their ruins
I've been loved by many corpses in those ruins
Many corpses loved me in many cities that walked inside my head
Hand in hand with many other streets
Every day you became a target at the corner of one of the walls of
      those cities
And every day I became a martyr
Standing right beside you
It made no difference whether it was at the corner of a wall in Herat
Or in Gaza
In Khorramshahr

Or in Lahore
Or inside a fairy-like girl from Kobani
Or in the wonderful memories of a boy's wet dream in Baghdad
I've been martyred so many times
Count me, you'll see
I've been martyred even more times than you
Once, you slept at the foot of a wall in Beirut
But me – I've been martyred

Oh, the nocturnes of the streets in my head
Oh, the sadness choking up the throat of the Middle East
Oh, the lamentations for the boys of my chest with the voices of so many
mothers

Start
Start
From ceaseless moaning in countless languages
From the inflamed wounds on endless bones
Start
Walk
Walk
Walk
My lover has gotten entangled in every language
He has become an immigrant in the throat of all accents
Oh, the streets in my head
My lover
Has become pregnant amidst countless sheets of paper
Has yawned in many faces but her sleep has been disturbed by the eyes of
        the moaning
Holding a lantern in her left hand and a tress of her hair in her right hand
My lover is standing straight on a path in the midst of

Are the winds blowing?

In the midst of lights

Are they smothered?

In the midst of rains

Are they raining green?

My lover has become miserable as a prostitute in exchange for a brief
smile

On a Pacific beach

Oh, the nights of the streets in my head

Lie down on the grave of metaphors

My lover has ached for centuries

The bruised vein of her thin body throbs

The loud mourning of her glance

Has gone on strike many times with blistered feet

My lover in the streets in my head

Merges with herself every Friday for a short collective death inside me

Half of me is planted inside her and the other half withers away

Every other Saturday, but

She has confessed to repeated falls

And on bloody Sundays of the Qandahar of her lips, her objections
demonstrate in the streets in my head

My lover is a twelve-year-old girl with the virginity of a gypsy's sad song

My lover is a prince, wondering about the path

that leads to a kingdom or the one that leads to caves with primitive
images

My lover – there are so many curses in her name, in the ancient identity
card of her geography

Many streets walk inside my head

I shove my hand into my selfishness

I seat you beside me

As if you've been my lover for years and months and I throw your light
      on me
More luminous than someone else's lover of years and of months
As if your veins are the red veins for my lips in my summer of agate and
      cashmere passion
As if my memories were only the same as yours
My lover of months and years
I will pluck you from the whole geography of the Middle East
From beneath the burqa of an Afghan woman or an Arab dishdasha,
      near me,
And I will shelter you in my bosom
In the huge borderless image of my body
My lover of years and of months
In a brief and compressed space?
I will exile you to a strange corner of my mind
I need this safety when you are out of reach
And you become a martyr with so many languages and strange accents
Oh, my lover of years and of months
I became ash in so many different ways
You won't remember
Sometimes my throat was slit by a blade
Sometimes in a mass suicide I exploded over you
Sometimes with my hair
And sometimes with the passion of my breasts, I was consumed in fire
Lover of the nights of the streets in my head
I have been several mass graves for you
My lover of years and of months
I have been several mass graves for you
Oh, my lover of years and of months

RODNEY SAINT-ÉLOI

Translated by André Naffis-Sahely

Rodney Saint-Éloi's poems in this selection are excerpted from *Récitatif au pays d'ombres / Recitative in the country of shadows* (2011), a book-long poem in four movements dedicated to Port-au-Prince, the largest city and capital of the author's native city, from which he had been absent for over a decade. While rooted in that city, these meditative lyrics also grapple with Édouard Glissant's concept of *Tout-monde*, or the Whole-world, allowing the author the examine his place in a globalised planet. This is Saint-Éloi's first appearance in English.

The Sun Suffers from Angina...

The sun suffers from angina
the headlines report
the healers beg the gods
the temples are devoid of prayer
no-one answers the roll call
children spit out the blood of hills
rap music splutters into a long wail
who among us drowns in their own blood
who among us is a shooting star
what chance?
the chance to save his blood
in the hollow of his heart
the chance to hug his dreams
close to the body of his cries
the chance to be a cloud unswept by the rain

Opposite: A man with black dreadlocks and short grey beard is speaking into a mic, wearing a white shirt and light grey blazer.

Facing the Sea...

Facing the sea
maybe I don't exist
I exist inside the parenthesis of fear
the fear of becoming that vexing word
when the sun stretches its arms
I turn into a grain of dust
I turn into a mortal thing
a man among men
the glowing red dawn of the islands
a flaw among flaws
a stone inside a house made of stones
a leaf that falls among fallen leaves
a fly hovering over the day's trash
a bee in the hope of the hive
it varies, day by day,
hour by hour
breeze by breeze
Facing the sea
facing the sun
facing the moon
my shadows expand far beyond my bodies
maybe I just don't exist
maybe I'm a scream that's still asleep

CAROLINA SCHUTTI

Translated by Jen Calleja

While I was Translator in Residence at the Austrian Cultural Forum
London I invited the author Carolina Schutti, whose dark and poetic
novel I'd loved and partially translated, to come to London to be in
conversation with the writer Joanna Walsh. Both travelled very far
for this intimate and riveting event, and I've always remembered
Carolina's warmth that bitterly cold Wednesday in February 2016.
In April 2021, Carolina wrote out of the pandemic blue asking if
I would like to collaborate on a poetry and translation project where
we would both write a series of poems and translate one another's
work. We agreed to use the phrase 'your eyes might be open, they
might be closed', something I said during an initial conversation,
as our starting point. The resulting poems were published in
December 2021 in *The White Review* and *manuskripte* (Graz)
respectively, the latter also accompanied by an excerpt of Carolina's
translations of my poems and a bilingual poem made of combining
lines from both our sequences. We're delighted that MPT have now
published an excerpt of my translation of Carolina's sequence, and
we're very grateful to the initiative Internationale Literaturdialoge
for funding our collaboration.

Your eyes might be open, they might be closed

when i was born
YOU CAN BE WHATEVER YOU WANT TO BE
was tattooed on my tailbone
and the finest slivers of carrot
were mixed in my mother's milk
so that everything would be
       as it should
and now i'm standing here
:
what do you want
and have
not got
the faintest
       idea

◆

and on opening my eyes
i see rust
       on my joints
it feasts through my pale skin
and i reason that
i should stop sitting still
       press bravery into my body instead
and as i rest my fingertips on my elbows

Opposite: A white woman with very short black hair and wearing all
black sits cross legged on a large white stone staircase. She looks directly
at the camera.

on my waist
on my knees
it occurs to me
    i could open my eyes
and on opening my eyes you are lying next to me
    your hand on my chest
    as if you could hold me back with it,
    preventing my escape even at the night
and while still sleeping it occurred to me
    i could just open my eyes
and on opening my eyes
i see your coffin
and in this coffin lies a book
in which you have written your life
i read it
without opening the cover
page by page
word by word
and i reason that
a word is only part of the truth
and sometimes not even that
and i read out loud
to check
    if the word would become more truthful that way
and it won't and it occurs to me
    i could just open my eyes
and on opening my eyes
i see a picture
the picture is of a face
yours

and i know it
and recognise you
and at the same time don't know
how the little hairs of your brows were sketched
and whether the left hand corner of your mouth is drawn down
slightly
or the right
or the way you're wearing your hair
or how old or young you are in this picture
and it occurs to me
　　　　i could just open my eyes
and on opening my eyes i see your hair
lying on the floor swept into a mound
and i see your clothes over a chair
and your shoes are nowhere to be seen
and i wonder
and open my eyes
and on opening my eyes i feel your lips on the nape of my neck
warm like before
and tender
　and i stare daggers
　　　　and though shadows weigh nothing
　　　　they are what
　　　　propel my courage into the strait

◆

everything resides in the dissolution
like in the primordial soup which i imagine as a
sea where the waves are painted
using blue 15:3 (CI 74160) and green 7 (CI 74260)

billowing images over the congealed ground crawling
animals that make the black lava
useful what can the thoughts be fed with
        i asked you and you said depends :

                                    ◆

don't commit yourself whatever you do
        optional
one word for a shrine
for a coffin made of armoured glass
this mobile of corpses, for
skin is nothing more than coke,
craving a hut
an oven
where the eternal fire smoulders

EPHREM SEYOUM

Translated by Yemisrach Tassew and Chris Beckett

As translators, we love this poem's description of Addis Ababa and
the flaneur poet hugging street corners and cafés, eyeing up the
beautiful girls! Piassa is the old Italianate area of shops, bookstalls,
cafés, while Bolé is much newer, brasher, the busy airport road
crashing through it, full of new shopping malls and hotels. The poem
captures this tension between an older, sexier Addis and the 'rainbow
make-up' quarters like Bolé, new but rather cold, so no love-bed,
instead a mourning tent.

One of the main problems translating Amharic is to convey
its punchiness: it has many plosive consonants, eg the poem's first
word (q'ech'in, meaning thin) starts with two plosives, so we begin
our translation with 'T-shirt' (a hard 't' sound) and continue with
as many alliteratives (belly button, Mehamud's Music shop etc)
as we can.

Is the narrator sympathetic to a Western reader today when the
male gaze is under such critical examination? We are not sure!
Ethiopian readers (mostly women according to Seyoum, who claims
to have sold over 40,000 copies of the book this poem appeared in)
find his narrator bold and refreshingly honest. The poem is written
in alternating 6 and 12 syllable lines (with some exceptions) which
creates a flowing rhythm to the poem, like the flaneur's gaze
wandering this way and that; so we have used 2–3 stress lines
and 4–5 stress lines to try and convey the same effect.

Saturday in Piassa and Bolé

Her T-shirt ends above
her belly button and her little waist,
a gold chain resting on
her breasts, a girl I've just seen by the road...
I wonder where she's going,
if a boyfriend waits
somewhere to cook her 7 eggs, 500 grams
of beef, yawning and
re-yawning, opening his book, leaving
his door open, checking
and re-checking his watch, not wanting
to drink coffee without her,
especially on Saturday...?

◆

she's gone and now I'm watching
4 young men by Mehamud's Music shop,
with something dodgy wrapped
in newspaper (chat leaves...?),
impatiently they order
food enough for 7 but in such
a rush they gulp their food
down silently, no chewing...I can guess
the reason why, it's
Saturday, you see, I understand!

◆

nearby, on the edges
of the neighbourhood, I see a dusty
field with flowers, children
singing, playing, skipping lunch, tummies
full of little games
and why? oh yes, it's Saturday

◆

this/that   left/right   I turn my head
from Piassa to Italian village,
thoughts pop up and others fall, the building
of my brain...construct/destroy...
today I have a date: you've come to lunch with me
at Yohimya, coffee at Tomoca's,
so we say and do the normal things
but I'm picturing you naked underneath your dress,
I say 'we shouldn't always meet
in the same spot, let's go to Bolé, there's
a great motel I know!'
OK, so we leave Piassa, reach Bolé
and find that Saturday
is different here, more dreamlilke...still, I think
that Bolé's girls in rainbow makeup
cannot match the lovely way you combed your hair in Piassa...
Saturday in Bolé doesn't look or feel
like Saturday in Piassa:
no lovebed in Bolé! instead, a mourning tent
stretched right across the road, across the day...
and you who came with me
say
follow me!

and hail a cab
and when we get to Piassa
we forget the Bolé tent because we're diving
in a sea of sunshine   joy
and music   whiskey   beer and laughing   dancing
dancing   laughing   dancing
why? because it's Piassa and it's Saturday!

THE FINGERS OF OUR SOUL

The Bodies Focus

RAYMOND LUCZAK

Prior to creating my ASL poem, 'Fire Onstage', I was a Deaf poet
working primarily in English and translating the poems into ASL for
performance on stage. When my Deaf friend Susan Jackson died, I
was quite bereft. She had done so much for Deaf theatre, and for my
own career as a Deaf playwright as well. I debated how to honour her
memory until it occurred to me that I'd never created an ASL poem
from scratch, as opposed to writing the poem in English for translation
into ASL. For the poem 'Fire Onstage', I decided to try using the same
handshape throughout the entire poem because why not challenge
myself to create something in a new genre, right? I created the poem
in ASL, wrote it down in ASL gloss, rehearsed it, videotaped myself,
and uploaded it to YouTube. (Recently I created another ASL elegy,
this time alternating two different handshapes, called 'Starsong', also
available on my YouTube channel.) These days I've been exploring
the idea of writing poems in ASL gloss (using English words and
ASL idioms in the ASL sign order), usually accompanied by the
poem in proper English. Just to be clear: there is no standardized
ASL gloss system at all, so it's been a fascinating process thus far.

The poems can be viewed at
YouTube.com/deafwoof

Opposite: A black-and-white headshot of a man with a short white beard
in a chequered shirt, looking directly at the camera.

Fire Onstage

For Susan Jackson (1945–2011)

[flat hands only]

Floor you-there fire

Me-watch, me-thirst, fire-fire

Hands-move, fire, hands-move, fire-fire

Group-people gather watch-together-you-move-back-and-forth-onstage

Finish you-there-came-to-me chat-chat-chat

You-there laid-back-laid-back-laid-back

My-hand-on-chest {JAW-DROP}

Floor wipe-clean no-no-no

Your hands you-there fire-inspire-fire cleaned-away?

No-no-no

Fire-fire-fire chest-press-over-heart small-fire-fire-fire.

ASHA KARAMI

Translated by Jo Dixon

I first came to Asha Karami's writing through a Poetry School course led by poet, editor, and translator Sophie Collins. Sophie presented us with an extract from Asha's poem 'DE ONSTAANGSGE-SCHIEDENIS VAN MIJN WEEFSEL', which I later translated as 'The Birth Story of My Flesh'. As we explored this poem, Sophie encouraged us to work with Laura Goldstein's provocation that translation is the 'constant act of the performance of reading, writing and displaying language to an audience'. Looking back at my translation now I can see the joy and physicality in that performance. The side bar on the page embodies my thinking line by line, moving through a 'painstaking focus on smallness [...] on patterns' to 'making the surface shine with rainbow annotations' to 'finding a fit that seems to measure up' and then 'dislodging' it. My commentary concludes: 'and I'm back-tracking, questioning all my decisions/ restarting.' Though there isn't a tangible representation of my translation process for the poem, 'licht/light', presented here, the dynamism and physicality of that first translation drove and was replicated in the second.

'licht/light' appears in the opening section of Asha's debut collection, 'Godface' (De Bezige Bij, 2019). The collection comprises fifty poems in Dutch split into five sections named after different areas of Taipei. Each section is then linked to an emotional state: delirium, agitation, aversion, apathy and euphoria. 'licht/light' appears in the section proclaiming agitation and as the poem oscillates between its images it gives body to that feeling.

Light

we meet at Leidsesquare, by Burger King
I can only get angry at computers, he says
when I ask about his politics

walking to the light festival
my fingers smell like salmon

with my back to a lighting rig
– squid projected onto a net overhead –
I examine him
the involuntary flickering of his eyes

I start to hear colours
if only I could listen at home, in bed
with Tramadol,
I could wash my hands too
                with lavender soap

I often act on impulse
   (mostly agree)
I often disapprove of others' behaviour and beliefs
   (neither agree nor disagree)
people find me ill-mannered and offensive
   (agree a little)

Opposite: A woman with dark wavy hair which is swept behind her is sat
down and looking off to the right. She is wearing an open-necked top.
Behind her is a dark wash.

the light shifts slowly towards me
if someone punches me in the stomach now, I'll throw up

he ignores my remark

I don't sleep at night
the bones in my fingers ache
a siren blares and fades

HOSHINO TOMIHIRO

Translated by John Newton Webb

At the age of 24, while teaching a gymnastics class, Hoshino had an accident which left him paralysed from the neck down. Two years into his hospital stay he started to write poetry, and to learn to paint with a brush held beneath his teeth. Two years after that he was converted to the Christian faith, which is a strong influence in his poems.

Hoshino's medium is the picture-poem. Japan has a long tradition of picture-poems in which the picture is not so much an illustration of the poem as it is a setting for reading the poem in, a practice born from a strong belief that the environment in which we read a poem will change our experience of the poem. There is also a personal emotional link for Hoshino between each poem and its accompanying flower.

He is counted in the 'naïve school' of Japanese poetry, where the word naïve has no negative connotations, but refers to a simplicity of vocabulary and grammar, and a tonal dominance of hope and joy (though often in the context of suffering). Though hope in suffering is a significant theme in his work, he has not written many poems specifically about his disability. The two featured here give an insight into his experience and personality.

Overleaf, left page: A painting of two flowers with leafy stalks on a white background. On the left is a rose. The flower on the right has looser petals. Above the flowers is a poem written in Japanese calligraphy.

Overleaf, right page: A line drawing on a white background of small coloured flowers sprouting from beds of white leaves on thorny stalks. Above them is a poem written in Japanese calligraphy.

筆を噛み砕きたい
時がある
槍のように
突きたてたい
時もある
さまざまな思いが
風のように　過ぎて
花を見ている

力ける人が
動かないでいるのには
忍耐が必要だ
私のように　動けないものが
動けないでいるのに
忍耐など　必要だろうか
そう気づいた時
私の体を　ギリギリに縛りつけていた
忍耐という　棘のはえた縄が
"フッ"と解けたような　気がした

Chewing my Pen

Sometimes
I want to pulverize my pen between my teeth.
Sometimes
I want to seize it like a spear
and impale things with it.
Various thoughts
blow through me
while I'm looking at flowers.

Patience

For a person who can move
    to not move
requires patience.
For a person who can't move
    to not move
who needs patience?
When I noticed this, I felt as though
the barbed rope we call patience
that had bound my body tight
was unbraided with one impetuous countermove.

LEVENT BEŞKARDÈŞ

Translated by Stephanie Papa

Levent Beşkardèş is a multidisciplinary Deaf artist who creates poems in French Sign Language (LSF) and Turkish. Born in 1949 in Eskişehir, Turkey and based in France, Beşkardeş came to Paris in 1980 with dreams of becoming an actor. He worked at a button shop to make ends meet while performing at the International Visual Theatre (IVT). Exploring the body's rhythm and its possibilities for expression are central to Beşkardeş's work. An accomplished performance artist, he approaches 'signs and gestures like choreography'. Likewise, gestures are conveyed in his visual art: 'Hearing artists have a number of outside influences. They often associate the voice with images, whereas I, a Deaf person, visualise hands with images', he notes. 'V' was translated into French by Brigitte Baumié, J. Carlos Carreras, Guillaume Gigleux, and Michel Thion, based on Beşkardeş's signed poem, with the help of interpreters. The French version echoes the poet's 'v' sign (used for both 'dance' and 'draw' in LSF) with inventive, alliterated 'v' sounds, evoking the playful, spontaneous gestures of both the dancer and the artist, who draws the former's movements. Beşkardeş's illustration and the French translation of this poem were published in *Les Mains Fertiles: 50 poètes en langue des signes* (Éditions Bruno Doucey, 2015), an anthology edited by Brigitte Baumié. It includes both Deaf poets and hearing poets, and is accompanied with performances in sign language on a DVD insert.

V

I see you dancevibrate before me
And I vergevacillate the pen that pivotjots on the blank paper
I see you danceblur in accelerated velocity
And I jolt the pen that quickly veervaults vaultveers

I see you waltz langvalourously
Come and go velvetvolleying on the paper
I see you Venus vanishdance
On my vividview paper of vitality

You give me your beauty life to life
Volantwave of our meeting of minds

You can watch Beşkardeş perform 'V' here: https://www.youtube.com/
watch?v=yOGzP2RcCNE&ab_channel=stephaniepapa

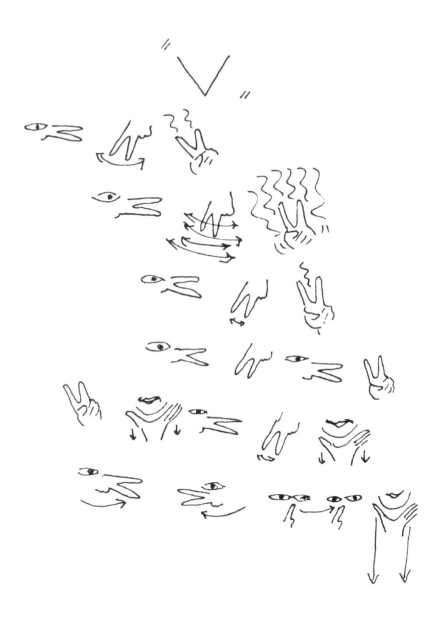

STEFANI J ALVAREZ

Translated by Alton Melvar M Dapanas

Filipino transgender writer and Saudi-based migrant (sex) worker Stefani J Alvarez writes from the tradition of the dagli, a genre which proliferated in vernacular publications even in the aftermath of the Philippine-American War (*Ang Dagling Tagalog: 1903–1936*, Ateneo de Manila University Press, 2007). The *Encyclopedia of Philippine Art* (Cultural Center of the Philippines, 1994) itself loosely defines said genre as 'vignettes or sketches' originating from the Tagalog *pasingaw*, Binisayâ *pinadagan/binirisbiris,* and Spanish *instantanea/rafaga*. My browsing of the 1900–1940s periodicals archive (Manila's *El renacimiento*; and Cebu's *Ang suga, El boletín católico,* and *Ang camatuoran*) confirmed my initial observation that this genre æsthetically ranges from oratorically highfalutin speeches to musings of a heartbreak (or in my and Alvarez's native tongue, 'maoy'), from societal treatises to narrative arc-less anecdotes of the quotidian. Such are poles apart from the dominant Euro-American short story form advocated by Iowa Workshop-schooled, Rockefeller Foundation-funded Filipinos who brought American New Criticism to our native shores in the mid-20th century.

As a báyot, precolonial 'male cross-dressers' (*Oxford Encyclopedia of Women in World History*, 2020) among a nomenclature of nonbinary/transgendered identities in the southern Philippines, Alvarez, through her œuvre, draws a parallel between two social constructs: *gendere*d bodies and *genre*d writings. In other words, she – author of two dagli collections, the latest one being *Ang Autobiografia ng Ibang Lady Gaga: Ang Muling Pag-ariba* (Ontario, Canada: Ukiyoto, 2021) – writes in, and more importantly, *queers,* a literary tradition that's without an equivalent in Anglophone writings.

NOTE: the poem 'Mutakabbir' refers to shisha, a molasses-based tobacco product, also called hookah or hubble bubble which is part of Saudi social custom. Tifayen is a double-apple flavored shisha.

A close shot of a young woman with straight dark hair in a light jumper, looking directly at the camera. Behind her is a white wall.

Mutakabbir

Our cage of a world revolves around in the middle of a desert.
Compared to Saudi Arabia and other neighboring Islamic countries,
Bahrain is an amusement park. The 25-kilometer bridge, the King
Fahad Causeway connects the two kingdoms. Bahrain is like Manila's
Luneta Park for both of us. *Filled with fun and thrill,* they say. Bar
hopping in Juffair. Shopping and movies at Seef Mall and City Center.
We can do a simple public display of affection. Holding hands while
walking at the lagoon, as warm as the qahwa arabeya coffee. Or him
hugging me as we gaze at the romantic Amwaj Island. I watch him,
and regret writes a verse.

> *we always bid goodbye*
> *like puffing*
> *to smoke shisha*
> *when will the ember become ash?*
> *when does the taste turn sour?*
> *we suck the sweetness of tifayen*
> *as the hashish intoxicates our souls...*

It's a different story at the other end of the King Fahad Causeway.
Hundreds of lashes are the punishment for the sin inherited from
Sodom. Such is the curse bestowed by the Kingdom of Saudi Arabia to
this kind of love. Denouncing our union. To them, Haraam is what our
chest smokes. I can evade from my god but our hearts can't escape.

I bottoms-up the sixth glass with a double shot Bacardi and coke.
I retched up like I was pregnant. I confessed my sins to the toilet
bowl. I vomited my insides. And I yowled and yowled like a cat.

Salam

And if love is just like mere lust which could be rinsed after a shower, I might wash my heart every day. The body can only thirst, but the heart bleeds. Because love is a disease. Fatal. A lot of people die because of it. But their bodies don't get buried. Only embalmed and mourned until they come alive again.

Just after maghrib, the fourth salah of that day. In solitude, grieving for my own corpse. Dead for over a month after Salman and I broke up.

Smoking by the front gate of my apartment, I wait for the prayer to end. All shops and establishments are closed during prayer time. Then from a distance, I see people coming out from the mosque. So I walk across the street heading to a bakalah or shop.

'Salam, sadiq...' an Arab man greets me upon crossing paths in front of the mosque.

'Salam...' I respond in Arabic.

We walk past each other. A few metres away, I turn around to look at him. He also glances in my direction. At the back of the mosque, we meet again.

AMIT BEN AMI

Translated by Lonnie Monka

In Israel, Amit Ben Ami is a fresh, rising voice in the world of poetry. He is also a social activist – part of progressive grassroots movements in Israel, and a member of an urban kibbutz. Though written in Hebrew, Amit's poetry is heavily influenced by the work of American poets – including Gertrude Stein, the Objectivists (especially George Oppen), and the L=A=N=G=U=A=G=E poets (especially Charles Bernstein). Given my own interest in the influence of American poetry on Israeli writers, it has been an amazing experience to help bring that American influence on Hebrew letters back into English. I hope that this cyclical cross-lingual influence only expands and gains momentum!

The poem presented here is from the first section of Amit's first full-length poetry collection, *Glass, Water* (Barhash, 2020). The section, titled 'Pictures', presents poems that utilise pared-down language that directly engage readers with curious features of day-to-day life and the playfulness of language. These poems present a contemplative attitude as well as invite us to join the meditation. Given the cross-cultural dimension of this translation, it seems fitting that the poem presented here revolves around the activity of eating food mid-flight.

Five Haiku Sketches

meal on a plane –
background noise conceals
my father's chewing

in-flight meal –
noise swallows the voice of
my father's chewing

in-flight meal –
almost silenced by the noise of
my father's chewing

eating during a flight –
from within the noise escapes
my father's chewing

meal on a plane –
overpowering the noise
my father's chewing

ÀNGEL TERRON

Translated by Rafael Cruz

This is a poem included in *Poetry of Science*, a bilingual Catalan-English anthology of the work of Majorcan poet and scientist Àngel Terron (Palma de Mallorca, 1953). He has a degree and a doctorate in Chemical Sciences and is currently a full professor of Inorganic Chemistry at the University of the Balearic Islands.

'Dirty Nails' is a poem based on a true anecdote of the Carmelite monks who educated Àngel Terron. They examined the schoolkids' nails all the time, searching for any signs of dirt. The poet has turned that anecdote into a reflection on how science, like poetry, is not something abstract and removed from messy reality, but an integral part of what it means to be alive.

As a translator, I take my cue from Borges, who said that to translate does not mean simply to transfer from one language to another, but rather to transform the text into another one, for each language is a different net thrown onto the world, with its own implications and associations. Having said that, Àngel Terron's poetry is very much influenced by the northern tradition. That's why I chose his work for my first book as publisher at Goat Star Books. 'Dirty Nails' flowed easily into English.

Dirty Nails

To Josep Lluís Pomar

At school, as a child, we kept having our hands checked, no dirt could ever be found in them. That review of hygiene and good manners was somewhat humiliating. The soil that was hiding there was sometimes the memory of a day spent in childhood's wild ways, investigating the brand-new world that opened in front of our eyes among the thistles and the insects of the fields.

Scratching and stirring up desire are typical tasks of the kind of research that stains the fingers of our souls. Researching about muscles and anatomy, Michelangelo Buonarroti used to remove the flesh of corpses, stripping them of skin, palpating and dissecting them, then he made drawings in Chinese ink of that lust to enjoy and feel. He always had dirty nails.

MARIA CYRANOWICZ

Translated by Malgorzata Myk

Maria Cyranowicz's work is associated with *neolingwizm* – language-oriented experimental poetic practices of a group of Warsaw-based poets, who signed their *Manifest Neolingwistyczny* in 2002. 'carefully (version 2.0)' appeared in the anthology *Queer. Dezorientacje*, co-edited by Alessandro Amenta, Tomasz Kalisciak, and Blazej Warkocki in 2021.

The text combines formal abstraction with a heightened emotional register, connecting apparently incommensurate qualities that Cyranowicz's expanded version of conceptualism upholds with both striking rigour and social empathy. Her poetics is largely based on sampling fragments of texts, including functional texts, and different discourses; for instance, political discourse. She transforms syntax to unseal fixed meanings and associations of words, exposing their paradoxical equivocality. These strategies foreground concrete forms of oppression and show power exercised on all levels of social life by means of language.

In 'carefully…', the activity of cutting hair emerges as a form of power wielded by the hair industry dependent on heteronormative standards of female and male haircuts. The 'species of the smallest care' is an ecological category, whose reversed meaning indicates that the LGBTQIA minority receives the smallest degree of care from the society guarding its beauty standards. The poet stages a casual yet intimate encounter of a hairdresser and her client against the extreme backdrop of totalitarian state machinery that immobilizes and arrests fragile bodies, refusing care to those who most acutely suffer effects of social conditioning. Throwing into relief subalternity of such counterpublics, in Nancy Fraser's sense of these terms, Cyranowicz's poetry becomes an oppositional ground where hegemonic discourses are contested.

carefully (version 2.0)

if a hairdresser then with a ring in her nose or in the brow precisely
    undefined so that the haircut does not torture again with her assurance
    of knowing perfectly well how I usually look carefully out of myself
    so that no woman or man could guess the secret hideout of my breasts
if questions then not quite how with trained fingers she is massaging my skull
    stimulating circulation of quivers descending into the uneasy body
    a caress I will never be granted by the welfare state
    working itself to the bone sweating to push stock prices upwards
if in this hall of mirrors aiming for my head like gunpoints
    redemption of my hair seems to be a punishment for falseness of the role
    enacted in the framework of femininity whose unproclaimed rules
    keep me at the edge of my seat thoroughly like bars of bolted cages
    where humanity shamefully hides a species of the smallest care

MIREILLE GAGNÉ

Translated by Riley Donlon

These poems are from Mireille Gagné's collection *Two Minutes to Midnight Before the End of the World*, a title that refers to the Bulletin of the Atomic Scientists' Doomsday Clock, created as an indicator of the world's vulnerability to catastrophe. In 2018, it reached two minutes to midnight, and in early 2022, the time was moved to 100 seconds to midnight. This collection of poems that evoke the apocalyptic and the tender at once follows two characters who grapple with what it means to inhabit their bodies and the world.

Throughout the translation process, I paid careful attention to the atmosphere of each poem. There is a consistent feeling of intimacy, as well as a sense of imminent disaster and ruin. Balancing these aspects while staying faithful to the French has been difficult and rewarding work.

Opposite: A woman with a straight dark brown fringe, wearing a black leather jacket and cat-eye glasses, is standing with her arms crossed against a wall of neat wooden planks.

The city seeps through every rift...

The city seeps through every rift
enters through the mouth
breaks teeth
spills blood
shreds the interior
as it goes
ravages everything

nothing remains
of her
or her ancestors
except an old church façade
on the verge of demolition

we'll build houses there
that the birds will mistake for trees.

Her patched-together fur...

Her patched-together fur
stretched out by innumerable litters
too loose on her shoulders
no longer holds
the world
falls to the ground.

On Abū al-ʿAlāʾ al-Maʿarrī, or What It Means to Be Blind and Vegan during the Islamic Middle Ages

By Salma Harland

As human beings, we inhabit bodies and we sustain them through food consumption. What we eat to sustain our bodies usually takes on all sorts of meanings, as it becomes closely tied to our sense of identity and culture as well as to how others perceive us. Arguably, this was not much different for tenth-century Arabs who lived during the Middle Abbasid era. For example, al-Maʿarrī (c. 973–1057) was a blind Arab poet and philosopher who eventually adopted an ascetic lifestyle that incorporated a strictly vegan diet, the latter leading him to be regarded as a heretic by his Muslim contemporaries.

Abū al-ʿAlāʾ Aḥmad ibn ʿAbd Allāh al-Maʿarrī, commonly known as al-Maʿarrī, was born in Maʿarat al-Nuʿman, a populous town in the Abbasid Emirate of Aleppo (modern-day Syria). At the age of four, he became blind after contracting smallpox, which left his face permanently scarred. 'Of all colours, red is the only one I remember', al-Maʿarrī says, 'for I wore safflower-dyed garments during my illness. It was the last colour I saw'.[1] Al-Maʿarrī proved to be a gifted child early in his life. By the age of eleven or twelve, he had already mastered poetry before pursuing other fields of knowledge, including linguistics, history, and hermeneutics. In 1007, an eighteen-month visit to Baghdad proved decisive to the way al-Maʿarrī chose to lead most of his adult life. Where the Abbasid cultured elite flaunted their wealth by holding lavish banquets and wearing ornate clothes, al-Maʿarrī took pride in his modest, humble demeanour: 'Where the benighted flaunt their best garments', he

---

1 Ṣalāḥ al-Dīn al-Ṣafadī, *The Comprehensive Book of Lives and Deaths* (Kitāb al-Wāfī bi-l-Wafiyyāt), pp. 63–4, my translation.

says, 'I am content with my common cotton rags'.[2] Blind, short
in stature, and regarded as physically unattractive by his
contemporaries,[3] al-Ma'arrī was a highly controversial figure
amidst the Abbasid elite and literary circles in Baghdad. Despite
being a well-versed polymath, he still was not a typical well-rounded
'refined man' (ẓarīf).

After he returned to Aleppo, al-Ma'arrī lived a reclusive, ascetic
life where he confined himself to his house for more than five
decades. In reference to his blindness and self-imposed isolation, he
came to be known by his self-made epithet 'the Double Prisoner'
(rahīn al-maḥbasain). In one of his poems, he says, 'Ask me not about
new tidings, bad as they may be, | for I am herein confined to these
three prisons of mine: | My blindness, my self-imposed isolation, |
and my soul's imprisonment in an ugly body'.[4] Out of moral duty,
al-Ma'arrī only wore simple garments and followed a strict diet in
which he abstained from all kinds of meat, seafood, eggs, milk, and
honey, only to list a few. In *The Comprehensive Book of Lives and Deaths*
(*Kitāb al-Wāfī bi-l-Wafiyyāt*), Turkic author and historian Ṣalāḥ al-Dīn
al-Ṣafadī (1296–1363) writes that 'lentils were [al-Ma'arrī's] dinner,
figs his dessert, cotton his clothing. His bed was made of rough wool
and he took papyrus for carpets'.[5]

What is now known and accepted as veganism was considered in
al-Ma'arrī's time an unnecessary or even an unacceptable form of
asceticism (zuhd) that comes in conflict with the teachings of Islam,

2 Ibid, p. 73, my translation.
3 In his poetry, al-Ma'arī's spoke in detail of his contemporaries' view both of
his blindness and chickenpox-induced facial scars, where they often said his
countenance was an eyesore not suited for elite circles. See *The Tinder Spark*
(*Saqṭ al-Zand*) and *The Necessities* (*Al-Luzūmiyyāt*).
4 Al-Ma'arrī, *The Necessities* (Al-Luzūmiyyāt), p. 213, my translation.
5 Al-Ṣafadī, ibid, p. 78, my translation.

the latter of which actively encourages its followers to consume animal flesh and by-products; seafood; and honey:

> O believers! Honour your obligations. All grazing livestock has been made lawful to you . . . Indeed, Allah commands what He wills.[6]

> Lawful to you is game from the sea and its food as provision for you and the travellers[7]

> The bees . . . . [t]here emerges from their bellies a drink, varying in colours, in which there is healing for people[8]

Both Muhammad's sayings (Ḥadīth) and biography (Sīrah) reiterate what appears in the Quran. Muhammad consumed the meat of sheep, goats, camels, cows, chicken, bustard birds, zebras, rabbits, and partridges, as well as seafood and milk. He also prescribed the consumption of honey as medicine on several occasions.[9]

All of this led many of al-Maʿarrī's contemporaries not only to shun him, but also to go as far as to call him a heretic, an infidel, and a Brahmin. In *The Orderly Book on the Histories of Nations and Kings,* Arab jurist and historian Ibn al-Jawzī (1116–1201) writes:

> [Al-Maʿarrī] did not consume meat, eggs, or milk for over forty-five years; he said harming animals is Haram[10] and he only took plants for sustenance; he wore rough clothes and

6 The Quran, 5:1.
7 The Quran, 5:96.
8 The Quran, 16:68–9.
9 See *Saḥīḥ al-Bukhārī,* hadiths 5680–1, 5684, and 5716 as well as *Saḥīḥ Muslim,* hadith 2217.
10 Haram, an Arabic term meaning 'forbidden' often used in Islamic contexts.

seemed to fast most of the time. . . . It seems that he might
have been a Brahman, for Brahmans do not regard the act
of killing animals as permissible, and they reject all the
messengers. Men of Knowledge have said he was a heretic and
an atheist, which clearly shows in his words and his verse,
and that he contradicted the messengers, found fault with
the [Abrahamic] religions, and doubted the [existence of]
afterlife.[11]

Almost a millennium later, al-Maʿarrī is still misunderstood and
heavily criticised by many Arab and Muslim scholars, which brings to
mind al-Maʿarrī's own words when he says, 'As if I am a word on the
tip of Time's tongue | laden with far-fetched meanings | That men
repeat over and over again | in a vain attempt to understand it!'[12]

Yet, many of al-Maʿarrī's works, both in verse and prose, have
gracefully stood the test of time as some of the most influential in the
entire Arabic canon, the most famous being *The Tinder Spark* (Saqṭ
al-Zand), *The Unnecessary Necessities* (Luzūm Mā Lā Yalzam), *The
Epistle of Forgiveness* (Risālat al-Ghufrān), and *Paragraphs and Periods*
(Al-Fuṣūl wa-l-Ghāyāt). *The Tinder Spark* is al-Maʿarrī's first known
book of poetry, amounting to over three thousand lines. It consists
of seventy-four long poems in which he speaks of various notables of
Aleppo and librarians of Baghdad as well as his views on life and
contemporary politics. Al-Maʿarrī further establishes his
controversial views on life and poetry in *The Unnecessary Necessities*,
also known as *The Necessities* (Al-Luzūmiyyāt), comprising nearly
1,600 short poems – one of which I have translated for this piece.
In this book, al-Maʿarrī alludes to numerous things he thought

11 Ibn al-Jawzī, *The Orderly Book on the Histories of Nations and Kings*
(Al-Muntaẓim fī Tārīkh al-ʾUmam wa-l-Mulūk), pp. 22-3, my translation.
12 Al-Maʿarrī, *Saqṭ al-Zand*, p. 198, my translation.

unnecessary for sustaining both life and poetry – hence the title – such as meat consumption and rhyme schemes, to list a few. *The Epistle of Forgiveness* came as a response to a letter sent to al-Maʿarrī by Arab grammarian and traditionalist Ibn al-Qāriḥ, who said that al-Maʿarrī was as much of a heretic as pre-Islamic poets. In response, al-Maʿarri wrote an intricate fable in rhymed prose in which he goes to Heaven only to find the pre-Islamic poets of Arabia. *The Epistle*, thus, has been linked to Dante's *The Divine Comedy*, with some arguing that the former might have inspired Dante to write his magnum opus. *Paragraphs and Periods* is yet another work of al-Maʿarrī's that was considered highly controversial by his contemporaries. In this collection of homilies in rhymed prose, which some (mis)took for a parody of the Quran, al-Maʿarri openly advocates anti-natalism and veganism, thus reiterating and complementing his *The Unnecessary Necessities*.

Thanks to inserting some orthodox passages in his work, al-Maʿarri successfully managed to evade prosecution, if not crude criticism and ridicule, dying at the old age of eighty-three. To this day, he remains an interesting enigma that still stirs argument and controversy, and whose surviving works superbly unravel the workings of a blind individual, offering unique insights into what it means to be embodied.

ABŪ AL-'ALĀ' AL-MA'ARRĪ

Translated by Salma Harland

An Excerpt from *The Unnecessary Necessities*

You are not of sound mind or religion, so come to me
   and I will tell you about the true righteous ways.
Do not eat what the sea bears out of vain cruelty
   and do not seek sustenance from lean carcasses
Or hen eggs that were rather meant to be their young
   than food for shameless men and women.
Do not torment the unsuspecting birds
   by usurping what they laid; verily, injustice is the root of all evil!
Leave honeybees the fruit of their incessant labour
   about fragrant flowers,
For they did not reap it for another to have
   or give away as charity and alms-giving.
I have washed my hands of all of this and yet I still wish
   I had done so before my hair grew grey.
My fellow-men, if only you would know the secrets
   that I have come to know and keep!
You have been led astray. Come, if only
   you consider what I have so far told you with humble spirits!
You have been led on by a corrupt messenger. Why have you never
   questioned what he proclaimed?
If only you uncover the facts on which your religion rests,
   you would find various matters that bring about shame and disgrace.
If you are wise, you would not douse your swords with blood
   or order others to butcher vulnerable creatures.
How I wholeheartedly admire those who curb their desires
   instead of living off the livelihood of some frail souls.

You have many other foodstuffs that are of finer flavours
    and that are genuinely halal to consume.
Consider Jesus, who never tortured a soul for worship
    and walked the Earth like a humble passer-by.

A close headshot of a woman with thin-framed glasses and long dark
hair grinning and looking into the camera.

DL WILLIAMS

As a poet who creates poems in English and BSL, how I translate them depends on which language the poem started in. When I create a poem in BSL, the English text tends to be sparse, as it's often intended to be spoken alongside the performance of the BSL poem and the aim is for people to focus on the BSL. In this case, the poem began in English, freestyling on the idea of 'crips' taking over a space, literally and figuratively, that has generally only been occupied by the healthiest of the healthy, in fiction and in real life. I wondered what it would be like if bodies that are hindered on Earth, where we have to fight for basic rights, were to be transported to a place where gravity wasn't an issue and the vacuum of space made sign language essential. When I come to translate this into BSL, there will be some additions where I add extra context for idioms in English that have no direct translation in BSL, but there will also be some beautiful visuals as some lines lend themselves well to embodiment and iconicity. Were I then to adapt this poem for a live performance in BSL, I would go back to the English text and edit it accordingly, to allow for the pacing of and more focus on the BSL. Thus showing how translations can become almost a conversation between the original poem and the new poem. Isn't creative translation amazing?

The poems can be viewed at:

We Shall Inherit Space

The meek may inherit the Earth;
the cripples will inherit space.

The deaf, the disabled,
the body shapes unsuited to gravity.
May we be as graceful in space
as penguins swooshing through water.

In zero G, who needs legs?
Better they take up less space
or none at all.
Who needs wheels or sticks when you're floating?

What about working near blinding light of the Sun?
Better if you're used to being blind.
Braille buttons, haptic instruments.
Space assistance dogs a bonus.

The silence of space may drive some mad;
not me.
In space, no-one can hear you scream,
but we can see you sign.

I suggest NASA starts a recruitment drive.
When do I begin?

TRISHNA BASAK

Translated by Mamata Nanda

Trishna Basak is a Bengali author from Kolkata, India. An engineer by profession, her early working life revolved around technology and fueled her intellectual and artistic interest in the role of technology and the natural world in women's lives, as well as the possibilities of cyber-feminism and eco-feminism. Her literary work bears testimony to the wounds of the contemporary terror-stricken world as well as the estrangement of technology-dominated relationships.

'Shelves Full of Books' is from Basak's poetry collection *Library, Shirt Khola* (2019) which means 'Library, the Shirt is Open'. The library functions throughout the collection as a symbol of womanhood; the form of the library reflects a woman's bodily reality in the world. 'Shelves Full of Books' playfully uses the metaphor of books and literature to stand in for female wisdom, experience and secrets. I was drawn by Basak's inviting tone in this particular poem – connecting women's history to themes of curiosity and investigation. I struggled with the second part of the second line, where the narrator is *wondering* if she has indeed let too much time pass in the form of a casual rhetorical remark. I wanted to remain as faithful to the original as possible but to me, the harshness of the question when translated into English didn't quite fit with the flow of the poem; it could be something more oblique rather than a direct enquiry. In the end, I was happy with my choice because it preserves the playfulness and the conversational register of the original.

Shelves Full of Books

For so long, I'd wished I could build a secret library
For the last thirty years in fact – is that too long?
Now, it has happened, books in every fold of my body!
Come reader, devour, letters and words and all.

There's religion on my nipples, philosophy on the golden triangle
History on my armpit, organic chemistry on the kneecaps
And light reading playing footsie on my fingertips!
Come reader, peck, letters and words and all.

ÓSCAR HAHN

Translated by G. J. Racz

'Tailor Shop', my translation of 'Sastrería' done in collaboration with the Chilean author Óscar Hahn, forms part of our third bilingual collection of his poems, currently under submission, and follows the publication of two earlier volumes of ours, *The Butchers' Reincarnation: Visions of the Nuclear Age* (Dos Madres Press, 2019) and *Poemas selectos / Selected Poems* (Nueva York Poetry Press, 2021). The piece itself comes from his book *En un abrir y cerrar de ojos* (In the Blink of an Eye) (2006). Hahn is sometimes called a 'poet of the fantastic', but his verse more accurately explores questions of being: a violin lying latent in a tree, genetically modified plants, mutant species, the experience of a newcomer in the realm of death, etc. Besides such ontic themes, Hahn's oeuvre also often entails a withering critique of mankind's cruelty in modern warfare, the adversarial nature of love, fantasias on historical figures, and man's apparent mad rush toward self-annihilation.

In 'Tailor Shop', Hahn's speaker contemplates death in ludic, somewhat macabre fashion, likening it impossibly to a suit of men's clothing he fears his body will grow into. Fond of the sonnet, Hahn still frequently composes poems in strict metrical and stanzaic forms. In 'Sastrería', his lines alternate between loose hendecasyllables and heptasyllables (so-called 'pie quebrado' or 'broken foot' meter), while I render this into English with iambs in varying line lengths (except for one unstressed syllable that closes the translation). Throughout, I was concerned with the poem's flow in the target language, employing contractions and opting for words other than 'and' (Sp, 'y') but for a use in the final line.

Tailor Shop

I've tried on death as if it were a suit
that's still too big on me for now

although I'm quite afraid
my body will begin to grow
until it reaches my death's size

when suddenly the clothes will fit:
the comfortable shoes
bespoke dress shirt

and suit that's made to measure

SAHERA KHAN

Translated by Sahera Khan, Irina Drytchak and Jamie Hale

'I don't care if it is repeated' is a poem in British Sign Language (BSL), by Sahera Khan, written with a tightly woven, repetitive structure. Within this, her attitude and mode of performance alters and shifts the tone and intensity of each signed repetition.

The original translation of this piece was by the author Sahera Khan – a Deaf BSL poet – and Irina Drytchak. When approaching this, I reworked some of the phrasing, but focused on capturing the motion and presence of BSL on the written page. It was important to remain true to the original, and I discussed intention and translation with Sahara and Irina during the process. Translating, I was aware both that the content spoke to my experience as someone who uses hearing aids and frequently has to request repetition, but also that I am not at all fluent in BSL, and did not wish to alter crucial elements of meaning.

There was a strong intention to remain true to Sahera's initial concept of the piece. Trying to capture the shifts in mood that flow through her performance was challenging on a static page. The initial frustration at the obliviousness of a hearing world becomes a joy in her own signing, and in slowly coaxing, persuading, and demanding the hearing watcher to understand and interpret her sign.

The repetition of the piece enables the non-signing viewer to slowly come to understand a portion of Sahara's meaning and intention even without captions or translation, and this visual translation was designed to accompany her process. The integrated QR code allows the reader to return to Sahera's original piece, bypassing the translation entirely – if desired.

I don't care if it is repeated
I don't care if it is repeated
I don't care if it is repeated
I don't care if it is repeated

I **don't care** if it is repeated

Look at my hands

〜〜〜〜〜〜〜〜〜〜〜〜〜 *¿what's that?*

My **sign**

understand?

I **don't care** if it is repeated

it is sign language

BE QUIET

〜〜〜〜〜〜〜〜〜〜〜 *for who?*

IT IS FOR EVERYONE

...BUT...

I am Deaf

and you could also be Deaf

I **don't care** if it is repeated

HOLD ON

our **rights**
our **culture**
our **language**

understand?

I **don't care** if it is repeated

stop

Look at my hands

¿tell me what's that? 〜〜〜〜〜〜〜〜〜〜

you nodded

My sign

u n d e r s t a n d ?

I **don't care** if it is repeated

it is **sign language**

BE QUIET

see?

it's a **beautiful** language

I **don't care** if it is repeated

one   more   time
look   at   my   hands
last   time   I'm   asking   you

¿what's that? 〜〜〜〜〜〜〜〜〜

YOUR SIGN

finally you understand

I **don't care** if it is repeated

LOOK

it is sign language

YANG XIAOBIN

Translated by Canaan Morse

Yang Xiaobin's poems like to reach for liberating or damning
epiphanies through absurdity, a creative resource he uncovers
through false contrasts and by collocating words that don't 'go
together' according to the habits of socialised language. Preserving
that strangeness requires being creatively hands-on with vocabulary
and hands-off with the logical aspect of syntax. Choosing words that
will shake the reader awake takes a certain intervention; I use 'foxy'
for *liànglì*, one of the many Chinese adjectives relating to feminine
and/or floral beauty, to communicate the source word's sense of
glamorous sharpness instead of resorting to an easier term (like
'glamorous' or 'sexy') that an English reader would simply pass by.

Meanwhile, allowing Yang's oftentimes dizzying train of reasoning
to achieve full effect requires recreating his double negatives, non
sequiturs, and strange anthropomorphisms as straightforwardly as
possible, in order to avoid accidentally making more 'sense' than
the source texts intend.

Opposite: A man with short black hair and thin-framed silver glasses,
wearing a dark polo shirt, is crouching and looking off to the left.

Swallowtail Butterflies

for Zang Di

At last I can count all the swallowtail butterflies
on my body. Just as lips are not tattoos, those wings
have drink-till-you-drop pimples that coo
before they start to rustle.

Though wind isn't as foxy as whistling, fine rains
will still drop into midnight, making happiness more worried.
If it continues this way, even sandstorms will pick up Beijing accents,
and completely ignore the springtime and acoustics
in a sneeze.

How many dizzy spells does it take to halt the hair's dance poses?
Or to stand on a summit and catch whiffs of fish-freshness?
Tonight, cherry blossoms chew up their ears –
by coincidence, water lilies also bite their fingers.

RAKA NURMUJAHID AMMRULAH

This poem was written in BISINDO, an Indonesian sign language, and translated into English and BISINDO gloss. BISINDO gloss is a written approximation of BISINDO. Before this piece, I haven't been fluent in poetry, yet I have actually written a poem. While learning with Okka, I discovered interesting ideas about representing myself as a Deaf person who is invisible in public society. Being an invisible person, it's surely not going to be easy, because hearing people don't know sign language, which is part of my identity that I'm proud of. So, representing sign language, I want to encourage Deaf people to learn how crucial it is, that it is something we should be proud of. I also want hearing people to know what sign language is and what the benefits to learning sign language are.

The poem that I wrote is for Deaf people and also for hearing people. I made it as simple as possible, to help hearing people understand what I want to say and sign. The piece represents how proud our Deaf community is. Another one of my reasons for writing a poem is that I want to help save future Deaf children who are born to hearing families who don't know sign language and Deaf culture. Surya Sahetapy – a Deaf activist – says that around 90% of Deaf children were born into and raised by hearing families who don't know sign language. That's an issue that should we be aware of, and we should create more ways to help them, to make sure they can learn sign language, to receive just as much as hearing children during their formative years. I wrote a poem that is meant to make an impact on them.

Sign Language

Written and translated by Raka Nurmujahid Ammrulah
from BISINDO into English and BISINDO gloss

We stare and sign
Sign language,
When we're diving, we are signing.
When we're blocked by the glass, we are signing.
When we're the noise, we are signing.
When we're so far, we are signing.
Sign language is an actual beauty,
Really.
Who am I?
This is: I am Deaf.
A signer.

Stare and sign
Sign language
Diving, we signing
Blocked, we signing
The noise place, we signing.
So far place, we signing.
Sign language.
Sign language beautiful
We signing.
Am I who?
Am identity who?
I'm a Deaf
Sign language.

LUCÍA BOSCÀ

Translated by Karen Elizabeth Bishop

In her 2019 book of poems, *Aphasias*, Spanish poet Lucía Boscà gives us a broken language to interpret a broken world. Here aphasia – loss of speech, an inability to make or understand language, the bodily breaking down of communication – becomes a way to describe and intervene in a world itself unspeakable. In this sense, aphasia speaks the world more authentically than any stable speech. It speaks in starts and stops, caesuras, blind spots, misidentifications, metonymies, layers, holes, gaps, minor lucidities that shine too brightly in an otherwise dark field. But for Boscà, these are not anomalies of language, but fundaments of speech so that speaking whole, non-aphasiac speech, becomes the strangeness, the impossibility in a world itself always coming apart. She calls out the comfort of whole sentences, sense-making syntax, and nouns that apply to reveal the constitutive, world-making rupture that language covers over. The poetics that emerges is both riot and return, revolution and homecoming.

Translating Boscà is to enter into a profoundly destabilising landscape of sound, image, and radical new combinations of object, self, memory, time, and dwelling. Like a scar that offers new flesh, her language gives the translator new material to work with. I have made up words, split images, reorganised syllables, dug up affinities, lost the thread, and taken refuge in sound. To translate speechlessness demands a remaking of language from the ground up. Here the collection's final poem, 'my body has lived', wherein the death of language becomes a rehabitation of flesh, utterance, fear, and desire.

Poem

My body has lived
death. In death are
unpronounceable languages.
Straight scatter when
the dead speak to me.
The voiceless light
tells nothing, waves that don't blossom
that say nothing because they
have nothing to say
and even so they say 'come' and 'return'
and I go down again,
beneath the skin and finally,
to be able to, at last, I can (,)
to be able to and birth and say what do they say they say:
'What of desire is there in fear?'
And without fear there is no
body, pronunciation and what's missing.

Opposite: A woman with dark brown hair in a raincoat is stood up on
a windy beach, wearing sunglasses and smiling. Behind her, the sky
is bright with only a couple of small clouds.

A photograph of a woman's face close-up on the left, with blank space on the right. She has short hair and looks directly into the camera.

MAYA WUYTACK

Translated by Harriet Jae

Maya Wuytack is a Flemish poet, director and 'embodied arts performer' whose work revels in sensory experience. She writes, performs and directs poetry films and stage productions which include dance, music and visual art and explore the poetics of the speaking body. Maya's poetry film debut 'Beyond the Body' won seven international awards at the Five Continents Film Festival.

As a disabled poet I relish the intense sense of freedom and physicality in Maya's work. The title poem of her recent collection, *Moederdicht*, evokes a sensuous tenderness which extends to the act of writing poetry itself. So I chose to retain the original title's neologism: 'moeder' means 'mother'; 'dicht' means 'close or intimate' and also refers to the noun 'dichter' meaning 'poet' and the verb 'dichten': to write poetry.

Whenever I was in need of inspiration in bridging the seemingly untranslatable, I would watch the poetry film of 'Moederdicht' (of which the English language version is forthcoming). Mesmerised by the strangeness and beauty of the film and the music of Maya's Flemish voice, I found solutions then arose.

Moederdicht

Do you know where light was born?
The first horizon?
The soft pink of the first day?
There where time arose,
where consciousness was cradled
in an ocean of sensation,
where breathless senses listened
to themselves.

A being
in whom I
can come into being:
Mother.

As infinitesimal cells
inside your self,
my self began –

my body broke out in you like a storm,
swarmed into form,
became human.

On your branches,
my little heartbeat
blossomed,
like secret singing swelling into song.

A bursting forth
inside the dark kiss
of your internal embrace
– like fruit, your growing flesh,
like ripening trust –

as you slowly sense
the truth of your transfiguring

and know your self
to be my swaying cosmos,
my personal sea.

Heavenly source
where I began
my earthly course of crashing, of landing.
Nine lavish months you sang
me into life,

then laid me on the lips of time
so I could rhyme with waves and stars.

Warmed by your sun,
I am the sum of your devotion.
Without your light, your sustenance,
my stories would have budded dead.

Instead, the language of your arms
was my first tongue –
soft sounds
inscribed like smiles

inside my skin.
Your tenderness
still clings to my limbs
like ink.

Inside the secrecy
of your flesh
you whispered your wish,
for so long singing
the heart inside your heart
into song.

This music dawned
before words.

EDWARD DYSON

Translated by Anthony Price

It had been a long while since I had looked over a piece of poetry, let alone written, or translated any. Yet, all it took was the small spark of an idea, and I was there again, flitting away the days obsessed with a piece of work. Well, I say work, but this was more a concept, an experiment that piqued my interest.

You see, what I haven't mentioned is that I'm disabled with a little-known condition as Spinal Muscular Atrophy Type 2. In a nutshell, this leaves my muscles extremely weak and unable to function correctly. This in turn means that I use a lot of adaptive equipment to do everyday tasks. One of the pieces of equipment is the Tobii EyeGaze which gives me PC access and allows me to use my eyes to select things on my PC screen. As part of its software, the EyeGaze comes equipped with a predictive text, on-screen keyboard whereby I select words, or letters with my eyes. For some, it takes some getting used to, but for me it just comes naturally.

The task that piqued my interest came during a conversation with a friend. They asked if I had ever thought about whether the words were suggested by the programming, or the words that I chose to use. In all honesty, I hadn't. It was just another tool to add to my arsenal. Needless to say, I began typing, trying to gauge how much I was writing and how much I was choosing from a limited selection. I started to wonder whether I was the writer, or if it was the computer. Did it improve my writing? Was my work stifled by the often slim choice? Answers needed to be found.

Below is the end result. As you can see, using the great poem 'The Typewriter' by Edward Dyson, the two poems have an air of similarity, yet, juxtaposed together, the words and structure change dramatically in some places, but in others are left unsullied. As for the last two lines, the predictive text just kept using the same words, which didn't fit the lines above, so in the end I thought it better to omit them. It's been a great project and I hope you enjoy it.

My Typewriter

I have a trim typewriter now,
They tell me none is better;
It makes a pleasing, rhythmic row,
And neat is every letter.
I tick out stories by machine,
Dig pars, and gags, and verses keen,
And lathe them off in manner slick.
It is so easy, and it's quick.

And yet it falls short, I'm afraid,
Of giving satisfaction,
This making literature by aid
Of scientific traction;
For often, I cannot fail to see,
The dashed thing runs away with me.
It bolts, and do whatever I may
I cannot hold the runaway.

It is not fitted with a brake,
And endless are my verses,
Nor any yarn I start to make
Appropriately terse is.
'Tis plain that this machine-made screed
Is fit but for machines to read;
So Wanted (as an iron censor)
A good, sound, second-hand condenser!

Predicted Poetry

I have a trim typewriter now,
They think that not one is better,
It makes a pleasing, rhythmical row,
And neat is every single letter.
I trick out stories by machine,
Dig par, and gags, and verses keen.
And lathe them off in manner slick.
It's so easy and it's quick.

And yet it feels false, I'm afraid.
Of giving satisfaction,
This message of literature by aid,
Of scientists traction.
For often, can't find what I need to see,
The Dashed thing running around me.
It bolts, and does whatever it may
I cannot hold the runaway.

It's not even been fixed with a break,
And endless are my verses,
Not any yarn I would love to make
Appropriately terse is.
'Tis plain that this machine made screen
Is only for machine to read.

BERNADETTE DAO

Translated by Andrew Sclater

Bernadette says that her poems like this one, from around 1990, were driven by 'rage pounding through my veins... for my country'. She implicates the authorities, the oppression of her compatriots, as well as her own impotence as sources of that anger. But its fuel is her intense love for her country, Burkina Faso, and her craving for the changes needed to ensure her society's survival.

At the end of her notes to me for this introduction, she adds '...then suddenly another me ('un autre moi-même') offers me a hand, becomes the echo of my deep pain across the seas, to let me be heard, in a different language from my own, far, far away from my country...!'

I was surprised, delighted, and moved by this acknowledgement. Some responsibility! Then, soon after, problems of cultural appropriation were foregrounded in media debates over the 'right' person to translate the poem Amanda Gorman delivered at President Biden's inauguration. As a white European man, I became uneasy about what I had done. So I suggested Bernadette might find a black African translator to take my place. But she insisted we carry on.

From the moment that her phone bleeped with my request for permission, out of the blue, we had got hold of something that delighted us both. Bernadette granted my request within the hour, in the middle of a wedding lunch in Ougadougou! I hope my translation of her work reflects the energy, spontaneity and passion of this leading Burkinabe poet.

Opposite: A woman with rectangular glasses stands with her arms down by her sides, dressed in a leaf-patterned top and headscarf. The trim of her top is decorated with flower shapes and she wears a necklace with a glittering square pendant. Behind her is a sandstone wall.

Future

'Come on, the sky's blue'.
                    -'But I'm too afraid'.
On the woman's ripe belly
                    There's a gun balanced
                    And a sharpened dagger's
                                    There too
                                    On the woman's ripe belly.
And I think of the girl who's yet to be born
                    Or maybe the son –
Of that first glance as it finds the gun
                    And the sharpened dagger,
        That first cry sharpening in pitch
                    And the mother going wild
                                    And the child gone.
And I think of the ripe belly
                    And these weapons of death
                                    On the ripe belly.
                    Horror tightens its hold on my heart
                                    And I think of tomorrow
With no tomorrow
                                    Of tomorrow's Fire and blood.
                    I'm afraid!
                    And the blue of the sky
Can't make the fear fade...

CHEN XIANFA

Translated by Martyn Crucefix and Nancy Feng Liang

Chen Xianfa was born in Anhui Province, China, where he still lives. Poet, essayist and journalist, his collections include *A Book on Death in Spring* (1994), *Past Life (2005)*, *Engraving the Tombstone (2011)* and *Poems in Nines* (2018), awarded the Lu Xun Literature Prize. His essays (in two volumes) are titled *Heichiba Notes*. I first read his work in the Bloodaxe anthology of Chinese poetry, *Jade Ladder* (2012). At the 2020 Cambridge Poetry Festival, I discovered more of his work as translated by Nancy Feng Liang. Since then, Nancy and I have been working together to bring Xianfa's 2018 collection, *Poems in Nines* to a wider Western readership.

Xianfa's writing registers the modern world's 'assault' on the individual's self and spiritual well-being. Part of that individual consciousness is a critical awareness of Chinese traditions. He writes: 'poetry is the dissolution and overwriting of the "known". The poem takes everything regarded as "accomplished" in the world and transforms it, through language, into something "unfinished", to create a newly liberated space'. 'Between Forms and Traces' is fascinated by 'oneness', or 'the same piece of clay in its differing forms'. It also suggests this poet's surrealistic streak: 'China's indigenous culture actually contains a strong current of surrealism which has long been overlooked and unexplored [. . .] In every really existing object there is a magical dimension, a "lost part" [. . .] traces of the gods, and a whole variety of distinctive emblems and symbols continue to be present to our lives'.

Between Forms and Traces

A four or five year old girl in a red cotton jacket
is riding on the broken head of a Buddha.
She chatters and sings,
oblivious to the fact that I watch.
These two figures,
in the twilight,
seem to be at war, one with the other,
at the same time both making a plea to become one.

How is it we love
the same piece of clay in its differing forms?
The primordial organism,
this, apparently variegated,
this single celled,
this hapless, indistinguishable rod.

The little girl will eventually throw off her red cotton jacket
and the Buddha break from the stone –
one thing happening after another.

The world's desolation
still some way from being widespread
and a little girl eating sweets runs like a warm current across me.

Opposite: A black-and-white photo of a man with short black hair in a
blazer, against a black background.

Consider our own lives,
once so unsettled,
eyes, there beside our own eyes,
in such abundance:
the eyes of birds of prey
as the cold wind is gusting over the treetops,
the eyes of its shrilling
and as the waters close over my head,
the eyes of the lake,
each and every single eye.

CSENGER KERTAI

Translated by Diana Senechal

When people call a poem 'musical', they usually refer to its rhythms, assonances, alliterations, rhymes, or other songlike qualities. While not songlike on the surface, Csenger Kertai's poems suggest and inspire music. It was through music that I first encountered Kertai's work: the musician and songwriter Sebestyén Czakó-Kuraly had set one of his poems to musical accompaniment, as part of a larger project in which various musicians took part. What makes these poems musically compelling?

The answer lies partly in their bare form and motion. Motion of body, spirit, and mind, motion in and out of the self, motion into a troubling question or a trembling leaf. Kertai's poem 'Hold' (Moon) has been set to music twice: by VUBalázs and Szántó Lili, in haunting blues-tinged electronica; and in a soaring, contemplative jazz rendition by the Hász Eszter Quintet. Both versions play with the sparseness of the words, imagining what lies behind and inside them.

Their images suggest music as well. Kertai's poem 'With Greatest Ease' moves nimbly from sewing to harvest to skiing to shuddering sunlight. A piano could play with this.

At its best, translation itself is a kind of musical rendition. Like the sunshine in 'Greatest Ease', it can make leaves rattle; like the blood vessels in 'Moon', it can 'tauten, tremble, and shine'. If it hits an essence, it resonates. The translator must honour the original poem but also take risks with it, because poetry itself risks. In translating Kertai, I find risk and honour.

A black-and-white photo of a man sat outside, with shoulder-length hair holding a smoking cigarette in one hand.

Moon

The moon shines on a dove's belly.
It carries my weight to you,
because this way you can bear the view
if the glance itself disappears.

See, it's easier this way. I don't rest,
I move from branch to branch;
my topsyturvy blood-vessels
tauten, tremble, and shine.

Who am I, if you come out of me at night,
taking what matters along?

With Greatest Ease

I feel your weight
as I weave from place to place on you
like thread in the eye of a needle;
I never take into account
that someone has died from this procedure,
but excitedly keep stitching your skin.
There are no real stakes here,
since the things you consider weighty mundane problems
I can start up again and again, with greatest ease:
the harvest, and how much the sun shines,
and whether you can put me aside
for skiing, summer vacation,
because I prowl back to you,
my face tweaked past recognition,
so that you will feel my weight,
but only like autumn leaves
that the sunshine shudders upon
if you go too close to it.

ZUO YOU

Translated from the Chinese by Yi Zhe

Zuo You has suffered from a hearing impairment at the age of six. Since then, he has been exploring sounds, eager to hear every day. His hope to communicate with the world has shaped his poetic practise. Zuo You writes with high accuracy to evoke feelings which strike home in the text, and to achieve self-transcendence. At times, his writing is insolent, modern, lyrical, direct, self-ridiculing.

I have been translating Zuo You's poems about sound, deafness, and fate since 2015. In a way, I become his ears and mouth, telling people a story about his soundless world with my own voice – the most challenging but exciting work for me. I hope my translation will make you have a different and deep grasp of sound.

Coincidence

Late at night,
I lay on the bed,
putting on
the long-disused hearing aid
at leisure.

Under the pillow,
the couple downstairs.
The moment I turned over,
they seemed to stop
making
a
noise.

Opposite: An illustrated headshot of a man with short hair looking
directly forward.

REVIEWS

Normal Things

Katrina Naomi reviews *Liminal* by Laura Fusco, translated
by Caroline Maldonado, Smokestack Books, 2020 and *Nadir* by
Laura Fusco, translated by Caroline Maldonado, Smokestack
Books, 2022

According to the United Nations, 82.4 million people have been
forcibly displaced from their homes (2020) 'as a result of persecution,
conflict, violence, human rights violations or events seriously
disturbing public order'.

While most have found hospitality in neighbouring countries,
some have travelled from Syria, Venezuela, Afghanistan, South
Sudan and Myanmar/Burma, among other states, to Europe.
Laura Fusco has worked in refugee camps in Italy and France;
her collections seek to give voice to refugees. Fusco's is a poetry
of witness, a poetry of reportage.

Both *Liminal*, winner of an English PEN Award, and *Nadir*, are
published as bilingual editions, in Italian and English. Caroline
Maldonado's translations flow, allowing Fusco's humanity and her
writing to make its impact. At the start of *Liminal*, Fusco states:

> The text uses writings by migrants and seen on banners/
> cardboard/walls/various materials, on television news and on
> the internet. Misprints and errors contained in the original have
> not been corrected but reported [...] the very idea of correction
> is contrary to the idea of the collection which [...] restores
> fragments of women's lives and stories.

Many of the poems find beauty among the desperation. In
'The Balkan Route', Sid 'washes | in the sky that runs in the puddle'.

Violence is frequently placed alongside some form of romance in a
poem: 'two of the military | throw themselves on top of someone left
behind'. A few lines later, we read:

> while the slip of a half-moon
> appears between MacDonalds the skyscrapers
> and the almond tree
>
> (From 'Refugees are survivor')

It's not always clear which country we are in, where the refugees
are fleeing from or which refugee camp is being referred to. I wonder
whether this is deliberate? There's a good deal of disorientation in
these collections, quite possibly Fusco is choosing to mirror the
situation refugees find themselves in.

Much of the poetry comes from refugees' own mouths. In 'Song
of exile', the language of reportage is lifted by what appears to be a
direct quotation, the use of italics adding to this sense:

> We've crossed hills and mountains,
> deserts and cities
> to say: *no more of our sons' eyes at the bottom of the sea.*

Unsurprisingly, the sea is a common theme: 'the still air tastes of
salt, | dysentery', from 'TV news', a title which doesn't do the poem
justice, and in which a woman can't sleep or drink, hasn't 'washed since
you were at sea [...] thirsty water in your mouth'. I found this reference
to the sea, from 'Backs against the wall!', even more impactful:

> the others populating
> the Mediterranean
> where a future's being written on the ocean floor

There's little to differentiate between *Liminal* (2020) and Fusco's 2022 collection, *Nadir*. Perhaps this is the point? Nothing has changed, the crisis continues. It feels a little churlish therefore to be raising the question of form in poetry when reviewing two collections on such an important issue. In many ways, *Liminal* and *Nadir* do a wonderful job, Fusco's writing bringing refugees' lives to the forefront, thrusting their hopes and fears, their plight, their common humanity before the reader. Yet, almost every poem in both collections is formed of one stanza. By refusing stanza breaks, a poet gives their reader fewer chances to look away, fewer chances to take a breath. In short, one stanza poems can force a reader to stay with the poem. So here, Fusco's use of form could be said to be a strong choice.

However, there's a sameness in the approach to the poetry which can feel monotonous. Poem after poem following the same path, with little to differentiate between them, other than length. There's little sense of 'play' in the writing, little use of line breaks – again this could well be mirroring the subject matter – but with greater attention to the possibilities of form and of variety in the poetry, these collections could have been stronger still.

Yet there are many surprises in the collections, notably the focus on technology. 'We can't live without free wi-fi' in *Nadir*, features a 'Britney Spears ringtone' and a demand for 'sky sport'. People in camps are shown throwing out:

> sofas, chairs, set fire to bedding to film a video and
>   post it, to protest, out of boredom

Elsewhere in the same poem, women are looking after their children and it is here, with the focus on trying to create some form of 'home' life, that Fusco finds truths which energise and illuminate:

To be normal and to do normal things
that is both women's fortune and their revolution.
And from normal things
comes the future.
Even here.

Reporters are everywhere in the camps and everywhere in the
poems. Fusco appears to be listening in to these interviews, and also
holding her own conversations: 'Today her mum told the TV | "*I have
big dreams for her, to study, become a doctor*".' (From 'I have big dreams
for her').

Hope is the counterpoint to despair in these collections.
A 15-year-old boy's monologue offers a wisdom beyond his years.
What I've taken to be his words ends the long poem 'I will live in
Rue la Marne' in *Nadir*, and concludes the collection in a way that
lifts him and the reader:

Dancing is a fragile joy,
but you must do it every day.
If you leave out only one day
you're leaving God out of your life.
When you dance and the bombs are falling
and flames set fire to the nights of your city,
you think that what you're doing won't put anything back in place,
but that's not right,
doing it
you change the world's plans
and your own.

'Why on Earth Does She Speak in Voices'

Dzifa Benson reviews *War of the Beasts and the Animals* by Maria Stepanova, translated by Sasha Dugdale, Bloodaxe, 2021.

Writing about the inclusion of the two long poems 'Spolia' and 'War of the Beasts and the Animals' in the foreword of her sensitive translation of Maria Stepanova's first full collection in English (also titled *War of the Beasts and the Animals*), Sasha Dugdale states that 'I shared her sense that these works, published together in 2015, were urgent and particular to the world now'. The two poems were written in 2014 and 2015 during the 'hot' war in the Donbas region, the killing-field of a war that took place between Ukraine and Russia, following Russia's annexation of Crimea.

Given the current escalation of hostilities between the two nations (which can be interpreted as the beasts and animals in lines like 'Russky or Ukranian | o you, whoever you are, in the neglected crossing place, | consider Vlas') the collection couldn't be more prescient in the urgency with which it speaks to this particular moment. It provides the English reader with a poetic glimpse into the 'corruptions and mythic untruths', as Dugdale puts it, that underpin this specific period of Russian culture and history. Conflating it with some of Stepanova's own Jewish family histories extrapolates the collection into an even deeper examination of Russian history as far back as the two world wars.

In its scrutiny of conflict and trauma and how that combines with culture, memory and myth-making – despite the inclusion of her own personal history – Stepanova's is a highly allusive poetry that suppresses a subjective viewpoint. Instead, it foregrounds the collective via the collage-like melding of fragments of language, which she subjects to immense pressure, culled from history (both familial and national), ballads, folklore, nursery rhymes, films, propaganda, social media, the words of other poets and other references whose idiomatic thrusts are beyond the scope of the English reader and, given Stepanova's penchant for associative experimentation, one suspects, are even beyond the scope of the lay reader of the Russian original. Perhaps this is why Dugdale has called the resulting collection 'a triangulation rather than a translation' in the foreword, which is especially helpful as a primer for the poetry itself. It may also be the reason why, unusually, Dugdale is given prominence as the translator on the cover of the book, which shows a detail of Hieronymous Bosch's painting 'The Flood'. Dugdale elucidates further in the foreword – 'much of it may be accessible to a highly literate Russian reader, some of it is Maria Stepanova's personal and private palette of associations and would not have been possible to translate without her help. [...] Stepanova's poem ('Spolia') demonstrates the poet's own endless lyrical complicity with war and the society and culture of a country at war. As a result, 'War of the Beasts and the Animals' is impossible to translate in a superficially faithful way. It would be possible to translate literally, word-for-word, but where would it get us, when nothing of this remarkable linguistic revelation would survive?'

That penchant for centring a multiplicity of voices and narratives, complicating attitudes to war and eliding blink-and-you'll-miss-them references within the space of a stanza, a line, a word and even a breath is not without its detractors among Russian critics. In typically defiant fashion, Stepanova repudiates their censure and throws down the gauntlet by incorporating it into the beginning of the poem 'Spolia', which also happens to be the beginning of the collection. 'Spolia' is the Latin word for 'spoils', as in 'the spoils of war' but it also calls to mind something that is spoiled or damaged. In this way, the poem can be read as a war against the poet and even a war within the

poet, illustrated by its modus operandus, the very fragmentation or
spoiling of language itself:

> totted up
> what was said
> amounted to

> she simply isn't able to speak for herself
> and so she always uses rhyme in her poems

> ersatz and out of date poetic forms

> [...]

> she's the sort who once made a good soviet translator

By the time the reader turns the page, Stepanova has taken that
censure and morphed into something altogether metaphysical,
uncanny and downright hilarious in sections:

> where is her I place it in the dish
> why on earth does she speak in voices

> (voices 'she has adopted', in quote marks:
> obvs anyone-without-an-I cannot adopt anything
> for anyone-without-an-I will wander, begging alms
> pretending to be a corner, a jar of mayonnaise, a cat
> although no one believes him quite)

> [...]

I'm the earth I send my cosmonauts floating

[...]

I won't even remain as air, shifting
refracting sound
fading with the light on the river's ripple
sucking the milk and vodka from still-moist lips

anyone-without-an-I
is permitted a non-i-ppearance wants libert-i

For Stepanova, this multiplicity of fractured voices and distorted
language is a resistance to a monolithic idea of Russian history and a
riposte to an authoritarian attempt to silence her and, by extension,
ordinary Russians. It's also a kind of metaphor for Stepanova's
attitude and stance among the Russian literati. Stepanova founded
the daily cultural website OpenSpace.ru in 2007, where she published
essays, criticism and reportage. When it lost its financial backing in
2012 because of government pressure on independent journalism
ahead of the Russian presidential election, Stepanova was forced to
shut it down. Not to be discouraged, she subsequently set up and is
the current editor of *Colta.ru,* Russia's only entirely crowdfunded
platform for arts and culture that is equivalent in format and tone
to the *London Review of Books.*

Stepanova is arguably Russia's most high-profile poet and
thinker. Although she is much younger, her stature, pedagogy and
prolificacy – ten poetry collections and three books of essays – are
comparable to a poet like the Nobel prize-winning Louise Glück
in the West. Stepanova has won many of Russia's most prestigious
literary awards, such as the Andei Beli Prize for poetry in 2005 and

the Joseph Brodsky Prize in 2010 and last year, her novel, *In Memory of Memory*, also translated by Sasha Dugdale, was shortlisted for the 2021 International Booker Prize. Despite all these accolades, the West has been incredibly slow to catch on to her particular brand of innovative poetry. It has meant that until now, the English-speaking world has been bereft of Stepanova's dizzying poetry which a critic called 'a carnival of images', and which adheres to the strictures of formal rhyming structures even while it pushes the elasticity of language to its limits. In the poem 'War of the Beasts and the Animals', for instance:

> no vember
> the cruellest month, the hoarsest mouth

Later on in the poem, the same method is deployed to even clearer effect of meaning and immediately after, a self-conscious meditation on language itself:

> all want con flag ration

> and here the iambs trip-trap: tetrameters chirrup
> but trip up on naked vowels
> and fall so far from europe
> bleeding pelts, they howl

I was curious enough to put 'vember' into Google's search engine to see if it threw up anything interesting. Right at the top of the return on my search: 'Vember means 'problems'. And the word November means 'no problems'. The Urban Dictionary had this: 'An adrenaline rush, something that makes you nervous, neurotic, uptight, etc.' While I can't attest to the veracity of either definition, they did give Stepanova's words another layer of meaning which seemed appropriate for this poem that commemorates the dead by way of a snippet from a nursery rhyme:

> this little piggy went to market
> and this little piggy froze to death
> and the landowner put a gun to his head
> and a black car came for the officer
>
> the greek in odessa, the jew in warsaw
> the callow young cavalryman
> the soviet schoolboy
> gastello the pilot
> and all those who died in this land

Elsewhere in the poem 'War of the Beasts and the Animals' we encounter another snippet – 'we happy few' – from a speech by King Henry V in Shakespeare's play *Henry V*:

> don't go back to mother
> don't wander the villages speaking
> from lips chalky white petrified
> *dear comrades brothers and sisters we happy few*

It elicits even more chilling layers of imagery after a casual Google search. 'We Happy Few' is also the name of an action-adventure survival horror video game which follows an imagined reenactment of World War II in which the protagonists try to escape a dystopia on the verge of societal collapse. Its inhabitants have been kept blissfully unaware about the truth of their world which enables them to be easily manipulated. I can imagine Stepanova alighting on this and delightedly incorporating this neat metaphor into her poem. After all, it is one of Stepanova's stated aims to use her poetry to resist government mandated manipulation of language, such as Putin's attempts to rehabilitate the reputation of Stalin, to fool the people. This seems to be borne out in lines like:

> this[fucking]country
> paradise sleeping in hell's embrace

And this, below, is the crux and raison d'etre of the entire collection and, I would argue, Stepanova's entire oeuvre in its recurring preoccupation with the intersection of memory, culture, history and mythology:

> the human body
> is not soap wearing thin to a hole
> in the scented water bowl
> nor is it ever wholly
> of the past, always of the here and now
>
> [...]
>
> and what was pining, barely alive
> shut away within its bony cage
> now floods into the dark recesses
> to happen again
>
> new life emerges when hope is no more
> and you stand there, empty-handed and unsure

Some of the cumulative effect of the experience (it feels more like an 'experiencing of' rather than a 'reading of') of Stepanova's poetry on the reader is akin to that familiar feeling of having a word on the tip of your tongue which your brain can't readily access in the heat of the moment. Other images, references and stimuli are pouring in so thick and fast that your brain doesn't have time to dwell on that elusive word before it's having to move on to the next set of words. Even so, the vestiges of the word nag away at you and cleave to meaning as you read on. This may well be Stepanova's intention. Her poetry isn't the linear, investigative querying of the past that attempts to join the dots like some temporal detective. Stepanova has said 'contemporary Russia is a realm of postmemory. I think it is a territory where poetry and politics still can meet each other on equal terms'. While I can't be absolutely sure what Stepanova means by 'postmemory' I'd hazard a guess that the fragmentary nature of her poetry attempts to enact the gaps in memory in a non-linear, circular way. Again, I think of the lines quoted above: 'nor is it ever wholly | of the past, always of the here and now.'

Stepanova's poetry isn't easy to parse even in its Russian original. Dugdale, who is herself an acclaimed poet and who has a deep knowledge of Russian history, literature and culture, has said that she was reticent for many years about attempting such a translation because it required a rendering that would enable the cultural idiosyncrasies of the original Russian to become legible in English. Then, it seems, the mistruths and manipulation of language surrounding Brexit here in the UK that echoed what Stepanova was trying to resist in Russia tipped her hand. Her careful attentiveness has produced an admirably sustained effort that is a tour de force introduction to Stepanova's urgently political poetry.

NOTES ON CONTRIBUTORS

ALIREZA ABIZ is a multi-award-winning Iranian poet, literary scholar, and translator. His most recent books include *Censorship of Literature in Post-Revolutionary Iran: Politics and Culture since 1979* (Bloomsbury, 2020) and *The Kindly Interrogator* (Shearsman Books, 2021).

AL-MAʿARRĪ (973–1057) was a blind Arab poet and philosopher.

STEFANI J ALVAREZ (she/her) authored *Ang Autobiografia ng Ibang Lady Gaga* (Visprint, 2015) and *Kagay-an, At Isang Pag-Ibig sa Panahon ng All-Out War* (Psicom-Literati, 2018), winner and finalist at the annual Philippine National Book Awards, respectively.

AMIT BEN AMI (1988), born in Jerusalem and living in Tel Aviv, is the author of *Kos, Mayim* (Barhash, 2020), and translator of lectures by Gertrude Stein (Dhak 2021).

RAKA NURMUJAHID AMMRULAH is a Deaf person from Indonesia, who was born to a hearing family that doesn't know sign language. Raka is a sports enthusiast, and loves movies, writing and drama serials. Raka's dream is to be an NBA head coach. Instagram: @rakana_10, Twitter: @raka10NA, www.liraka10.blogspot.com and http://rakanurmujahid10.medium.com/

TRISHNA BASAK is a Bengali author based in Kolkata. She has published numerous poetry collections, short stories, novels and essays and translated works from Maithili, a tribal language of India and Nepal, into Bengali. Basak is joint secretary of Kolkata Translators' Forum and has received several of India's highest literary grants and awards.

KHAIRANI BAROKKA is a disabled, Minang-Javanese writer, translator and artist, whose work is presented widely internationally. Her latest book *Ultimatum Orangutan* (Nine Arches) is shortlisted for the Barbellion Prize.

CHRIS BECKETT's latest collection is *Tenderfoot* (Carcanet, 2020). He also edited and translated with Alemu Tebeje *Songs We Learn from Trees*, an anthology of Ethiopian Amharic Poetry (Carcanet, 2020).

DZIFA BENSON is a multi-disciplinary artist whose work intersects science, art, language, the body, ritual and criticism. She is a Jerwood Compton Poetry Fellow 2021/2022.

LEVENT BESKARDÈS is a poet, actor, director, and visual artist. He has performed at international festivals for Deaf artists. He won the Honorary Prize of the Grand National Assembly of Turkey in 2010.

KAREN ELIZABETH BISHOP is a poet, translator, and scholar. She teaches literature and directs the Critical Translation Studies Initiative at Rutgers University. Her poetry collection *the deering hour* is published by Ornithopter Press.

LUCÍA BOSCÀ is a poet and professor who lives in Valencia, Spain. Her 2014 *Ruidos* won Spain's prestigious Premio Poesía Joven Félix Grande. *Aphasias* was the last collection she published before becoming a mother.

JEN CALLEJA is a British-Maltese writer, literary translator from German, and co-publisher at Praspar Press, a micro-press for Maltese literature in English and English translation.

GEET CHATURVEDI is a Hindi poet, novelist and essayist. He has authored two collections of novellas, three poetry collections, and two of nonfiction. His work has been translated into twenty-two languages.

MARTYN CRUCEFIX's *These Numbered Days,* translations of poems by Peter Huchel (Shearsman) won the Schlegel-Tieck Translation Prize, 2020. Forthcoming: a Rilke *Selected* (Pushkin Press) and essays by Lutz Seiler (And Other Stories).

RAFAEL CRUZ is a London-based writer and translator. He has recently founded Goat Star Books, a publishing house specialised in poetry translation to and from English. https://goatstarbooks.com/

MARIA CYRANOWICZ (b. 1974) is a Polish poet, literary critic, and teacher. Author of five poetry volumes, most recently *psychodelicje* (2006) and *den.presja* (2009). Co-editor of two anthologies *Gada !Zabic? Pa(n) tologia neolingwizmu* (2005) and *Solistki* (2009). She lives in Warsaw.

BERNADETTE DAO writes poems, short stories, and teaches in Burkina Faso. She has held ministerial posts in former governments. Her prizes for poetry include the French Prix Jean Cocteau (1995).

ALTON MELVAR M DAPANAS (them/they) is author of *Towards a Theory on City Boys: Prose Poems* (Newcomer Press, 2021), assistant nonfiction editor at *Panorama: The Journal of Intelligent Travel, Atlas & Alice Literary Magazine,* and editorial reader at *Creative Nonfiction.* Find more at https://linktr.ee/samdapanas.

JO DIXON is a scholar-practitioner and lecturer in creative writing at De Montfort University (Leicester). Her debut poetry collection, *Purl* (Shoestring Press), was published in July 2020.

RILEY DONLON is a student, poet, artist, and literary translator living in Birmingham, Alabama. Time, identity, and memory fascinate her. Her work appears in *carte blanche, Chautauqua,* and *Aura.*

IRINA DRYTCHAK is a Director of Sign for All Community LTD and a British Sign Language Interpreter. She is a CODA (Child of Deaf Adults) and has worked within the deaf community for several years. Her company, 'Sign for All Community' provides awareness and accessibility for D/deaf families. www.signforallcommunity.co.uk

PRIYANKA D'SOUZA /PINKA POPSICKLE is a visual artist, art historian, and writer from Mumbai, India, working with Mughal miniatures, early modern natural history, and the concept of '*ajai'b*' (wonder). Instagram: @pinkapopsickle @restingmuseum.

EDWARD DYSON (1865–1931) was an Australian journalist, poet, playwright and short story writer.

DU FU (712–770), also known as Tu Fu, is widely regarded as the greatest of the classical Chinese poets.

MIREILLE GAGNÉ (b. 1982) is a poet, novelist, and author from Québec, Canada. She has published several books, including four poetry collections with Éditions de l'Hexagone.

ANITA GOPALAN is the recipient of a Fellowship from the Indian Ministry of Culture and a PEN/Heim Translation Fund Grant. Her work is in AGNI, PEN America, Poetry International Rotterdam, etc.

ÓSCAR HAHN is one of Chile's most renowned poets, the author of more than twenty volumes of poetry and collected works. Hahn's most recent books in translation are *The Butchers' Reincarnation* (Dos Madres Press, 2019) and *Poemas selectos / Selected Poems* (Nueva York Poetry Press, 2021), both translated by G. J. Racz.

JAMIE HALE is a disabled poet and theatre-maker from London. They are one of the 2021–2022 Jerwood Poetry Fellows, and their work explores the body, nature, the mortal and the automated. They have performed in places including the Tate Modern and Barbican Centre. Their first pamphlet, *Shield*, was published in 2021 by Verve Poetry Press.

SALMA HARLAND is an Egyptian-born, England-based literary translator who works between Arabic and English. Her translations have appeared or are forthcoming in *Ancient Exchanges*, *ArabLit Quarterly*, *Medievalists*, and elsewhere. www.salmaharland.com.

SHOOKA HOSSEINI Born in Tehran, Iran, Shooka Hosseini has published two collections: *The Earth Was a Political Planet* (2015) and *The Streets inside My Head* (2020). Her first collection won second prize in the prestigious Shamlou Poetry Awards in 2016.

HARRIET JAE lives in Ghent, Belgium. Her poems are published or upcoming in *Poetry Wales*, *Stand*, *The Rialto*, *Mslexia*, *Poetry Salzburg*, *Harana Poetry, Acumen* and elsewhere. Longlisted in the 2021 *Mslexia* Poetry Competition, she was awarded the 2021–22 Poetry School scholarship for a disabled poet.

ASHA KARAMI writes poetry, prose, plays and essays, and collaborates on poetry films. She is a doctor in Amsterdam. Her poetry debut, *Godface* (2019), received three award nominations and a Dutch Foundation for Literature grant.

CSENGER KERTAI (b. 1995) is a Hungarian poet and the author of two poetry collections. A number of his poems have been set to music. He lives in Budapest.

SAHERA KHAN (she/her) is a Deaf Muslim and BSL (British Sign Language) user, a writer/creator, artist/actress, filmmaker, and youtuber. She is also a poet, who has been widely published and performed across the UK and in Rotterdam. Her website is www.sahera1.tumblr.com

NANCY FENG LIANG is a bilingual poet and translator, living in the USA. Translations into Chinese include Thoreau's *Wild Fruits.* Her poetry collection, *Qi Cun Tie,* is published by Taiwan Showwe Press.

RAYMOND LUCZAK is the author and editor of more than 25 titles, including *A Quiet Foghorn: More Notes from A Deaf Gay Life* (forthcoming from Gallaudet University Press).

LONNIE MONKA is a Jerusalem-based poet and Phd student (researching David Antin's talk-poems). He founded Jerusalism, a non-profit organization promoting Israeli literature in English. His work can be found online.

CANAAN MORSE is a literary translator, poet, and graduate researcher of ancient Chinese literature at Harvard University. His translations of Yang Xiaobin have appeared in *The Baffler, Solstice Review, Circumference,* and elsewhere. His translation of Ge Fei's novel *Peach Blossom Paradise* was a Finalist for a 2021 National Book Award.

MALGORZATA MYK (b. 1975) teaches North American literature at Lodz University. Author of *Upping the Ante of the Real: Speculative Poetics of Leslie Scalapino* (2019). Her translations of the avant-garde poetry of Leslie Scalapino, Lisa Robertson, Kevin Davies, and E. Tracy Grinnell appear in various Polish literary magazines. She lives in Warsaw.

ANDRÉ NAFFIS-SAHELY is the author of *The Promised Land: Poems from Itinerant Life* (Penguin UK, 2017) and editor of *The Heart of a Stranger: An Anthology of Exile Literature* (Pushkin Press, 2020). His second collection, *High Desert*, will be published by Bloodaxe Books in 2022. He edits *Poetry London* and teaches at the University of California, Davis.

MAMATA NANDA is a former academic based in London who has always loved reading poetry, and translating between Bengali and English. She is the first official Bengali translator of Maya Angelou's collected poems (Parampara Books, Kolkata, 2020) and is working on Sylvia Plath's poems.

KATRINA NAOMI's most recent collection is *Wild Persistence* (Seren, 2020), which was followed by *Same But Different* (Hazel Press, 2021) co-written with Helen Mort. Katrina is learning Kernewek (Cornish).

ANDREW NEILSON is a poet and essayist. He co-edits the digital poetry journal *Bad Lilies* with Kathryn Gray.

STEPHANIE PAPA is a poet and translator living in France. Her work has been published in *LOST*, Verve Poetry Press anthologies, *The Stinging Fly*, among others.

ANTHONY PRICE is a 37-year-old male residing in Canterbury, UK. An avid reader and film fanatic who always wanted to be a writer, he was first published at 15 in a poetry anthology and since achieving his MA in Creative Writing at Canterbury Christchurch University, has had several short stories published in e-zines, along with two published novels and two anthologies. His horror anthology *Tales of Merryville* is available in e-book format on Amazon.

G. J. RACZ is a professor at LIU Brooklyn, a former president of the American Literary Translators Association (ALTA), and review editor for *Translation Review*. His rendering of plays by Pedro Calderón de la Barca, Lope de Vega, Miguel Cervantes, and Sor Juana Inés de la Cruz appear in *The Golden Age of Spanish Drama: A Norton Critical Edition* (2018).

ZACK ROGOW is the author, editor, and translator of more than twenty books or plays. His ninth book of poems is *Irreverent Litanies* (Regal House Publishing, 2019). He is also writing a series of plays about authors and serves as a contributing editor of *Catamaran Literary Reader.*

RODNEY SAINT-ÉLOI is a Haitian-Canadian poet and anthologist who runs the publishing house Éditions Mémoire d'encrier. He was made a Compagnon de l'Ordre des Arts et des Lettres du Québec in 2019. His latest project, co-written with Yara El-Ghadban, is *Racists Have Never Seen The Sea* (2021).

CAROLINA SCHUTTI is an award-winning Austrian writer of prose, poetry and plays. Her writing has been translated into sixteen languages. She lives in Innsbruck.

ANDREW SCLATER is a Scottish poet currently living between France and Norway. His work has appeared in *Poetry Review, The Dark Horse,* and elsewhere. He translates from French and Norwegian.

DIANA SENECHAL is the 2011 winner of the Hiett Prize in the Humanities and the author of two books of nonfiction as well as numerous poems, translations, essays, and stories.

EPHREM SEYOUM was born in Addis Ababa. He has published short stories, philosophical articles and two CDs of poems with music. His collection *Feqir ezih bota fegeg bilo neber* (Love Smiled in this Place) came out in 2013 to great acclaim.

FARZAN SOJOODI, former professor of semiotics and linguistics at Tehran University of Arts, is an Iranian literary critic who has authored many books and articles in the areas of theoretical semiotics, cultural semiotics, critical semiotics, and literary criticism.

YEMISRACH TASSEW is a poetry-loving commercial lawyer working in trade and investment advisory services in Ethiopia. She was involved in translating many of the poems which appeared in *Songs We Learn from Trees* (Carcanet, 2020).

ÀNGEL TERRON (Palma de Mallorca, 1953) is a Majorcan poet and scientist. He has a doctorate in Chemical Sciences and is currently a full professor of Inorganic Chemistry at the University of the Balearic Islands. *Poetry of Science*, a bilingual Catalan-English anthology of his work, is available from Goat Star Books. https://goatstarbooks.com/

HOSHINO TOMIHIRO (1946–) has written 13 collections of picture-poems, drawn with a paintbrush in his mouth, and is one of Japan's most widely read poets. His work has been displayed in galleries around the world

JOHN NEWTON WEBB has had poems published in various magazines. You can read his work and mini-essays on Japanese poetry at johnnewtonwebb.blogspot.com. He lives in Sapporo, Japan, where he is the pastor of a church.

DL WILLIAMS is a deaf queer poet working with British Sign Language and English. They have performed around the UK including at the Scottish Storytelling Centre, Wales Millennium Centre, the Barbican and the Albert Hall, as well as in America and Brazil. They have most recently been published in *What Meets the Eye?* (Arachne Press, 2021), a bilingual anthology of deaf poets. DL's bilingual poetry collection, *Interdimensional Traveller* is forthcoming with Burning Eye Books. They are the current MPT poet-in-residence.

MAYA WUYTACK is a poet, director and embodied arts performer, whose books include *Nothing Chronic (Except Love)*, *Moederdicht* and *Ontbreekbaarheid*. With her 'partners in creation', she founded POST.TRAUM.Collective, an interdisciplinary artistic collective.

CHEN XIANFA was born in Anhui Province, China. He has published four poetry collections and two collections of essays. Awards include the Chenzi'ang Poetry Prize (2016) and Lu Xun Literature Prize (2018).

YANG XIAOBIN was born in Shanghai and took part in China's avant-garde culture movement as a student in Beijing in the 1980s. He moved to the US in 1989, where he earned a Ph.D. at Yale and taught before moving to Taiwan. He has published several collections of poetry, and is considered one of the most important Chinese-language poets today.

ZUO YOU is a poet and columnist. His poems often appear in major Chinese literary magazines, some of which have been translated into English and published in western literary journals.

YI ZHE holds an MA in English Language Education at the University of Reading (with Distinction). He has published in *Westerly, Poetry New Zealand, Acumen*, and *The Malahat Review*.